D0952649

The Beaux Arts Trio

Also by Nicholas Delbanco

About My Table, and Other Stories
Group Portrait: Conrad, Crane, Ford, James, and Wells
Stillness
Sherbrookes
Possession
Small Rain
Fathering
In the Middle Distance
News
Consider Sappho Burning
Grasse 3/23/66
The Martlet's Tale

THE BEAUX ARTS TRIO

Nicholas Delbanco

WILLIAM MORROW AND COMPANY, INC.
New York

Chapter II appeared in *The Bennington Review*,
number eight, and Chapter III in *Harvard Magazine*,
January-February, 1984.

Library of Congress Cataloging in Publication Data

Delbanco, Nicholas.
The Beaux Arts Trio.

1. Beaux Arts Trio. 2. Violinists, violoncellists,
etc.—United States—Biography. 3. Pianists—United
States—Biography. I. Title.
ML421.B42D4 1985 785.7'0092'2 [B] 84-1125
ISBN 0-688-04001-2

Printed in the United States of America

First Edition

1 2 3 4 5 6 7 8 9 10

BOOK DESIGN BY ELLEN LO GIUDICE

AUTHOR'S NOTE

I first heard the Beaux Arts Trio perform in the summer of 1962. The concert took place in Cambridge, Massachusetts; I was courting the cellist's daughter. We were married in 1970 and spent much of the next year in Europe; for one month, as a kind of honeymoon adventure, we followed the Trio through Germany. I remember grand hotels in Hamburg, Bremen, Berlin, and Munich—charming halls and houses in Würzburg and Tübingen. For the shorter distances, we rented a Volkswagen van, and I played chauffeur. It was one of violinist Isidore Cohen's first tours with the Trio; he had recently replaced Daniel Guilet. Aurora Greenhouse accompanied her husband, which she does only rarely and for "special" trips. So there was a sense of celebration, a shared freshness to the time; we visited museums and parks and shops and monuments, ate and drank continually and well.

My memories, however, are of how hard they worked. I was twenty years the junior of the Trio's junior member and fell asleep exhausted every night. The pace was unremitting, as was the schedule; when not onstage they rehearsed. They played a Beethoven cycle in Munich—three concerts—and remained for four calendar days. The intervening night there was a party in their honor; this was the Trio's night off. When not driving, we took trains and planes; the Frankfort airport grew familiar. By the end of the second week—or so he assured me—I had heard all of Cohen's jokes. The Trio had surely heard mine. By the end of the month, when my wife and I said thank you and good-bye, we were dizzy with recurrence and welcomed the last flight. We returned to our little house in Provence; the idea for this book was born there.

It has been a long time a'borning. The Trio have performed some fifteen hundred concerts since, and their eminence has solidified into preeminence. In the houses of the world where chamber music is heard or performed, they are a household word. I do not want to exaggerate. By comparison with movie or rock-and-roll or sports stars, they remain anonymous; there may still be airports where they may not be met. But the history of the Beaux Arts is more than coincidentally coeval with the rise of piano trio ensembles in our time, and to celebrate the one is to consider the other.

The sequence of what follows may take some explaining. If not a "musical" arrangement, it nonetheless attempts to shape a whole greater than the sum of the component parts. The performers are fond of describing their enterprise in just such a way, and I have followed their lead. The first chapter contains a narrative of the Trio's career and achievement; the third offers a detailed description of a single concert, what goes on "behind the scenes." The fifth chapter focuses on a recording session in Switzerland, at La Chaux-de-Fonds. Interspersed, in chronological order of the interviews (and stretching over several years), there are chapters devoted to the individuals: Bernard Greenhouse—Chapter II; Isidore Cohen—Chapter

IV; and Menahem Pressler—Chapter VI. Chapter VII describes a concert tour in France.

Four appendices follow. The first is a round-table discussion of interpretative strategies and ensemble issues (a discussion led by musician and author David Blum.) Next comes an extended transcript of the musicians' response to the performance problems in an agreed-on text: the first movement of Beethoven's *Geister* Trio, Op. 70, No. 1. There is an itinerary for a representative concert season, and a Discography.

Certain themes recur. One of them is the subordination of the ego. The "face" of the Beaux Arts is hardly featureless, but it is a collective face. I have therefore not included what might have been germane to another kind of composition: the names of their grandparents, or an analysis of their furniture or politics. I have not included—except where functional—their recipes or reviews. My principal task, happily, has been to listen.

Throughout I have attempted to keep my own voice to a minimum; this book describes a trio, not a quartet. It therefore feels appropriate to call the musicians by their surnames, not their first. The first-person pronoun figures in these lines more often than hereafter—but it would be coy as well as misleading to pretend I was not present on the road. Where there is repetition—intrinsic to the life they lead—I have retained it, if at all, as "leitmotif." Where their viewpoints differ, I have let the differences stand. But there have been few of the latter, and this introduction is a note of thanks.

The members of the Beaux Arts Trio, singly and collectively, proved unstinting in their responsiveness; as were their families. Hattie Clark, Tom Johnson, Volker Straus—

indeed, all who figure in the story—provided help; my indebtedness, implicit in what follows, should be made explicit here. This was a collective undertaking from the first phrase to the last. At several stages of composition, I sought and received advice from, among others, Stephen Becker, Alan Cheuse, Thomas Delbanco, Richard Elman, Joan Gardner, Jeffrey Levine, Jonathan Levy, Joe McGinniss, and Jon Manchip White. John Hawkins, Martine Mizrahi, and Gail Hochman performed the several offices of agentry from their several offices; the last named in particular steered me through straits. Livia Gollancz and James Landis, at Victor Gollancz and William Morrow, were splendidly supportive editors. David Blakiston of Columbia Artists Management, Inc., did yeoman work in their archives, unearthing dust-covered sheets. Of David Blum's assistance, more will be said in Appendix A; he helped us willingly and much. My thanks go to the C. F. Peters Corporation for permission to quote from Menahem Pressler's unpublished article, "Why Play Chamber Music?," and to *Clavier* magazine for permission to quote from an interview with him—some paragraphs of which I have, in effect, folded into Chapter VI. Peter Clancy of Philips Records provided the material for the Discography (Appendix D); brief citations are acknowledged in the text.

My father played the cello and my elder brother the violin; I struggled with the piano, then the viola as a child. We had chamber music evenings at home, and my exposure to the literature came well before I could read. But whatever ear I have I owe to the far finer ears and musical education of my wife, Elena; this book would not exist without her. Its faults alone are mine.

Chapter One

On July 13, 1955, the Beaux Arts Trio of New York performed at Tanglewood in Lenox, Massachusetts. This was their official debut, but prepared for at short notice; they had not been scheduled for the Berkshire Music Festival. The Albeneri Trio had been slated to perform, but a member of that group fell sick and they were forced to cancel. The Beaux Arts Trio of New York were therefore a substitution; they played an all-Beethoven program.

The festival conductor, Charles Munch, had known Daniel Guilet. He came backstage to greet the violinist and to make apologies for a previous commitment that would make him unable to stay. He remained, Guilet remembers, until 2:00 A.M. "The beautiful part," as Menahem Pressler recalls, "is that Munch came backstage. Before we played he said, 'Boys, I'm glad to greet you here. But I have to leave during intermission. I have a rehearsal early tomorrow morning. You will forgive me, but I wish you good luck.' Then he stayed to the end and was thrilled."

He was also generous; he promised to engage the Trio yearly thereafter at Tanglewood. And, for publication, he gave them an important piece of praise: "The marvellous musicality of these three artists has been unknown in trio playing for many years. They are worthy successors to the last great trio—Thibaud, Casals and Cortot." Two eminent soloists also weighed in. Zino Francescatti wrote, "I have just heard the Beaux Arts Trio in Tanglewood and enjoyed tremendously the perfection and artistry of this admirable ensemble . . . a great ensemble with great artists." And Robert Casadesus put it succinctly (if with a soupçon of Gallic reserve): "The finest Trio I have heard in America."

Casadesus' friendship with Daniel Guilet had been consequential in the group's formation; they had rehearsed at his home. He had recommended them to Arthur Judson of Judson, O'Neill, and Judd, a division of Columbia Artists Management, Inc.; "To Casadesus," says Guilet, "we owe everything." Then Arturo Toscanini heard them at his house in Riverdale and said, "Fine chamber music, with impeccable taste and musicianship . . . an inspiring experience." (To Guilet, who asked him what he thought of Bernard Greenhouse, the maestro responded, "*Che bella voce!*") The group was safely launched.

We rarely know when making it that a choice may prove momentous—that a momentary impulse will matter later on. We discover only after the fact a turning point once passed. A phone call made or not returned, a meeting turned convivial by the quality of sunlight or the wine, a coincidence remarked upon until it seems preordained: of such stuff careers are built. Later on it may seem clear that so-and-so did such-and-such when the time was ripe. But anniversaries commend the accidentality of things, not so much our intention as luck.

And intention can prove difficult to reconstruct; thirty years thereafter, our sense of the anticipated future feels long since in the past. "History" is less a prospect than a retrospect; we don't assume we're making history when we make a concert date. The beginning of the Beaux Arts Trio was a casual, offhand enterprise; none of the principals guessed, in 1955, what it would entail. Guilet was, by all accounts, the moving force; he gave the Trio impetus and shape. His experience of chamber music was both large and long; in Europe he had been a member of the famed Calvet Quartet. He hoped to give the ensemble his name, as he had done with the Guilet Quartet several years earlier. But the literature is, after all, that of a piano trio, and the violinist's name was insufficiently important to override the claims of balance. Nor did "Guilet, Greenhouse, and Pressler" have a commanding ring. Briefly, they would call themselves "The Beaux Arts Trio of New York." This had the appropriate French flavor for Guilet, yet located the musicians in America. There was a short-lived "Beaux Arts Quartet"—with whom they did not wish to be contractually confused. When the Beaux Arts Quartet disbanded, however, the Beaux Arts Trio returned to and retained their present name.

Guilet knew Greenhouse first; they had played together in a piano quartet. He had heard Pressler also, and they joined forces for studio recordings. As Pressler remembers it, Guilet came to his apartment for an impromptu performance of a Mozart trio—with the cellist Frank Miller. "And I was practicing the Schumann Quintet, and Daniel said, 'I can work on that with you. I know that piece very well.' And we sat a little bit, and he showed me what was done in the piece; obviously he knew it well, magnificently well . . . And one day there was a performance for MGM [Records] of the *Carnival of the Animals;* Guilet was the contractor, and I, in order to earn money, played the celesta in the recording. And Bernie played *The Swan.* Which he played beautifully. And somehow it was arranged that we would play together, and we did."

That arrangement took some time. A proposed series of Mozart recordings (for MGM Records) failed to work out.

Uncertain as to the prospect of a career in America, the pianist decided to settle again in Israel. With his wife and infant son, he returned to Tel Aviv. Meanwhile, Casadesus persuaded Arthur Judson that Guilet should form a trio; Pressler, too, was managed by Judson, O'Neill, and Judd. Greenhouse had a separate management (Herbert Barrett, Inc.) and a reputation as a soloist; his manager attempted to dissuade him from this new projected role. But things fell into place. Guilet remembers that he and Greenhouse were "in the listening booth at MGM . . . And Ed Cole said, 'How would you like to call Menahem? In Tel Aviv.' We did. He had just come in from shopping; he did not have time to put his steak in the icebox, he was already on the boat. . . ."

Pressler had not bought a steak, but his recollection concurs with Guilet's. "I was to play with the Israel Philharmonic that night. But we have a little boy, and I went on my way out to buy some milk. When I come back, my wife says, 'There was a phone call for you from New York; you're to call back.' I thought she was making a joke. I called, and Ed Cole said, 'How about coming back for three weeks; we will have some concerts.' I looked at my wife and said, 'Fine, why not?'"

Their early publicity reprinted early praise. The flier for the first season contains biographies of the Trio, and studio portraits. The three men stare at the camera, looking lean and soulful; except for the soft, shaded background, these could be passport photographs. Guilet wears a bow tie and Pressler a pompadour; Greenhouse has slicked-down hair. From having to practice five hours a day, Guilet says, he himself went bald by twenty-seven. . . . The brochures provide much information and only slight hyperbole; they can serve as introduction to the personnel by 1955. They are, in order, as follows:

DANIEL GUILET (pronounced *Gee-lay*) is almost equally famed in Europe and America as a soloist and as chamber musician. Born in France, he attended the National Conservatoire in Paris, studying and playing public performances with Jacques Thibaud and Georges Enesco. He concertized extensively on the continent, making guest appearances with the major orchestras and playing as a member of chamber music groups before he came to the U.S. in 1941, where he organized a new Guilet Quartet which played the length and breadth of North and South America and Cuba. In 1944 he was chosen as a member of the NBC Symphony when it was especially created for Toscanini, in 1951, became Concertmaster of that orchestra and still holds that position with the Symphony of the Air, as the NBC Symphony became known upon Toscanini's recent retirement. He has played as soloist under such conductors as Toscanini, Perlea and Cantelli, has given recitals in all the major cities of the U.S., has recorded for Concert Hall, Vox and Columbia records, and has generally been acclaimed as one of the finest soloist and ensemble musicians of our time. He plays the beautiful "Earl of Darnley" Stradivarius, dated 1712.

BERNARD GREENHOUSE captured the attention of the music world when he made a 1946 Town Hall debut of which Virgil Thomson wrote in the New York Herald Tribune: "Bernard Greenhouse is a mature musician and an impeccable executant. If you can imagine a whole evening of cello music without one false note, one groan or one scratch, you can also figure out why the hall was full of cellists. The news had obviously gotten around that the boy is good." Formerly a fellowship student at Juilliard, Greenhouse went to Europe in 1946 for an audition with Pablo Casals which turned into two years of study with the great Spanish master. Wrote Casals: "Bernard Greenhouse is not only a remarkable cellist but, what I esteem more, a dignified artist." Since then Greenhouse has won an enviable reputation as one of the major interpreters on his instrument, with appearances in most of the major cities of both Europe and America, in recital, with orchestra, with chamber music ensembles and with recordings for Columbia, RCA Victor, Concert Hall and the American Recording Society. In this country, in addition to his annual tours, he is on the faculties of the Juilliard and the Manhattan schools of music. He plays the famous "Visconti" Stradivarius cello, dated 1684.

MENAHEM PRESSLER, the brilliant young Palestinian pianist, was born in Magdeburg, Germany, but fled with his family to Israel when Hitler came into power. He began his professional career in his adopted country, and jumped to international prominence when he won the Debussy prize at the age of 17, after flying from Tel-Aviv to San Francisco especially for the contest. Embarking on his first American tour, he was soloist five times with the Philadelphia Orchestra, and was immediately awarded an unprecedented three year contract for several appearances each season with that famous symphony. He has since appeared also with such orchestras as the New York Philharmonic, the Cleveland Orchestra, Indianapolis Symphony, National Symphony in Washington, D.C., etc., in the course of annual nation-wide tours, and has recorded for MGM records. He returns from another series of European appearances—in Scandinavia, Israel, Turkey, Greece and France—to join Messrs. Guilet and Greenhouse for the initial tour of the Beaux Arts Trio. Mr. Pressler plays the Steinway piano.

That, then, is what they had accomplished. Guilet was fifty-six years old, Greenhouse thirty-nine, and Pressler thirty-one. Some of the data would change. Guilet acquired the "Hrimaly" Stradivarius—and, later, a Guarnerius—in place of the Earl of Darnley; Greenhouse replaced the "Visconti" with the "Paganini" Stradivarius (ex-"Countess of Stanlein"). The G string of the Darnley had been overpowering, and the two "new" instruments made a more even match. Guilet still mourns the loss of his "large" violin, Greenhouse remains devoted to the Paganini cello, and Pressler continues to play the Steinway concert grand. The latter's biographical ascription, "Palestinian pianist," was soon replaced by "Israeli." And he was older than seventeen when accorded the Debussy Prize, since he was born in 1923 and came to America after the war. By and large, however, the claims made by Columbia Artists were accurate—and the acclaim followed quickly.

In mid-October 1955, the Trio embarked on a forty-five-city North American tour, under the aegis of Columbia Artists Management, Inc. (CAMI). Greenhouse remembers that first season as containing eighty concerts, seventy of them "community concerts." (A community concert is prebooked by a management, which contracts to furnish music more or less the way a caterer supplies food. There will be some indication from the "host" as to the fare desired—operatic selections, say, or a woodwind ensemble—but the ingredients are purchased by the catering agency. This meant, in effect, that the Trio need have had no prior bookings in order to have work; CAMI kept them busy from the start.) Their New York debut came at the Frick Collection—on Sunday, January 22, 1956. They also performed at the Ravinia Festival near Chicago, on July 29, 30, and 31 of that year. The files at CAMI bulge with reviews, and a sampling will suffice. There is a repetition-pattern to superlatives, and we may confine ourselves to the response at Ravinia.

On July 30, in the *Chicago Daily News*, Irving Sablosky wrote, ". . . They played not just expertly but with a feeling for chamber music's style and atmosphere that turned Ravinia's big pavilion into a remarkably cozy place for listening . . . They sound as if they've played together always. There aren't half a dozen chamber groups on the stage these days who play with the kind of individual freedom and group integrity that distinguish the Beaux Arts . . . Each player seemed to pour himself completely into his music, and apparently by a wondrous coincidence the three combined perfectly—supported each other, learned from each other, matched and enhanced each other . . ." The next day he continued, under the heading TRIO AT RAVINIA KEEPS SPARKLING: ". . . The Beaux Arts Trio's Ravinia Festival concerts had the same kind of sparkle and liveliness that distinguished their debut . . . The Beaux Arts

Trio have something special to offer in the way of chamber music playing . . . an ensemble happily matched and finely polished as few ensembles ever are. Each of them plays expertly and with zest, and they go together seemingly without giving up any of their individual spirit—yet, with a perfect agreement in detail of phrase and feeling that [give] evidence of the most meticulous preparation . . . Breathtaking!"

Roger Dettmer, on July 31 in the *Chicago American*, wrote, "An exalted program . . . The Beaux Arts Trio was a towering ensemble one hopes can become a fixture on the local musical scene. All they, who are its members, do is instinctively and expressly musical—superbly congenial tempi in relation to musical substance, a communal way with phrasing that verges on the incredible, and string tone breathtakingly matched. A quite extraordinary trio . . . Together they give altogether memorable and quintessentially musical performances [and] rare pleasure . . ."

The title of that day's review by Seymour Raven, in the *Chicago Daily Tribune*, was: BEETHOVEN, BY BEAUX ARTS TRIO, AT BEST. He wrote, "The Beaux Arts men have pooled their talents all to the strength of chamber music, not to what is mistakenly regarded as a 'compromise' of artistic notions . . . No comments can prepare one for the pleasure that arises from listening . . ."

And under the headline TRIO GIVES BRILLIANT CHAMBER CONCERT, Felix Borowsky wrote in the *Chicago Sun-Times*, ". . . what was achieved with these works was so wonderful it may confidently be declared that, in all the years of its chamber music concerts, Ravinia never has put forth one which in perfection approached that of this performance. Here were three first class artists whose united musical sensitivity was extraordinary, whose oneness of thought and expression was almost uncanny, and whose beauty of tone and phrasing was, it seemed, inimitable . . ."

It is not, of course, merely a result of good luck or good auspices that a group succeeds. Pressler had to learn the repertoire. He was, self-confessedly, the least experienced of the Trio in chamber music playing: "I was introduced to it with blood, sweat, and tears. We took it very seriously; we started rehearsing and working in Wellfleet [on Cape Cod, Massachusetts, where Greenhouse has a summer home]." For the ensuing summers, they moved to Bloomington, Indiana, as faculty members of the University of Indiana School of Music there. Guilet and Pressler still reside in Bloomington—and all three remember those first six or seven summers as crucial in "making a face."

Guilet, at eighty-four, speaks with decisive asperity of those early years. His voice is high and quavering, but he is a practiced *raconteur*. Asked to talk of his association with Gabriel Fauré, he says, "I was a kid, and he was not a kid. I came from the canteen at the Conservatoire, where you eat for one franc, which was very dear to me. And there was Gabriel Fauré. Usually when you said to him, '*Bonjour, maître,*' he didn't answer—and children take for granted that, if a person doesn't answer, you don't have to always say hello. But he stopped me and said, 'You.' And I said, 'Yes?' And he said, '*Vous savez qui je suis?*'—'Do you know who I am?' And I nodded, '*Oui.*' 'Who?' 'Gabriel Fauré.' 'Why don't you say hello?' he asked. So I looked at him and said, '*Bonjour, maître.* Hello.' That was the whole conversation . . ."

With Greenhouse in Wellfleet, in August 1983, Guilet is less laconic. He delivers his opinions with panache.

"Well, I will say this to you, which is true from my heart. I had a great kick playing together with you, and with Menahem. We had to work together to come to that point; I am glad that I gave in in many things, you gave in in many things. . . . When I was younger the only attraction for me was to be a soloist, because he stands alone, there aren't three people taking the bows. . . . Facility has nothing to do with what you learn, because if you have facility you have the tendency not to study. . . . It is more pure to play quartets, because it is one instrument of sixteen strings. The trio is three soloists playing, which have to have the same heart, the same breathing, and the same ideal. If they have that, they will play trio beautifully . . ."

He and Greenhouse reminisce about the past, the long car trips in American cars that Guilet called "mastodons." When they saw a trailer, Guilet would always say, "Oh, look, that man is carrying his living room." When Pressler first arrived from Israel, he sported a felt hat. Guilet made him throw it away. "He looked like a rabbi," he says. "Two string players, and a rabbi." Fearful of Greenhouse's driving, he would plead, "Don't put me in the scenery." The men mimic each other, delighted. They then sing part of a round: *"J'aime l'ail, j'aime l'ail. Et moi, l'oignon, et moi, l'oignon"*—"I love garlic; me, I love onion."

There is an edge to his opinions, still, and characteristic hauteur. "Everybody wants to shine—including critics. But the critics have a tendency, when somebody's very good, to look for the little fault. But when somebody plays with a lot of faults, they look for what's good—'Oh, that was wonderful, that F sharp.'" And of an associate, "I liked his playing, yes, but also he played like a pig." Once, coming offstage, he turned to Pressler and said, "It could have been better. But it couldn't have been faster . . ."

Guilet announced his retirement one year before it came to pass. At the end of the 1968–69 season, he would be seventy years old, and there were increasing demands on the Trio's time. His ear hurt, his kidneys, his leg . . . He gave his junior colleagues the opportunity to dissuade him; they did not do so. Greenhouse and Pressler embarked on a search for a third member of the Trio and, after some months, settled on Isidore Cohen. He accepted. This was a painful period for Guilet and left a bitter aftertaste; it is never easy to see oneself replaced. He had been the guiding force in the early seasons and the best established of the personnel; though he left the Trio voluntarily, it was not without recrimination or regret. The mechanics of transition are simple (new press releases, new recording contracts, etc.), the emotional nexus, complex. An office memorandum, dated December 9, 1968, begins with the *fait accompli*: "As you know, DANIEL GUILET will retire at the end of the 1968–69 season and in his place will be the distinguished chamber music violinist, ISIDORE COHEN." Pressler and Greenhouse became the senior members of the group, and Cohen—who has by now performed and recorded the Trio repertoire more often than Guilet—the Johnny-come-lately. Listeners continue to compare the two, lamenting or delighting in the shift.

For the early seasons—in community concerts throughout America—the men played solo set pieces to render the program attractive. They ran through a small bestiary, from *Flight of the Bumblebee* to Saint-Saëns's *The Swan.* Here are some sample programs. In 1957, for the Community Concerts of Canada, they offered a program that began with Beethoven's Trio in E flat, Op. 1, No. 1, and ended with Mendelssohn's Trio in C Minor, Op. 66. In between, however, Guilet and Pressler performed Fritz Kreisler's adaptation of Tartini's *Variations on a Theme of Corelli,* Debussy's *Clair de Lune* and William Kroll's *Banjo and Fiddle.* Then Pressler performed Chopin's Etude in E Major, Op. 10, No. 3, and the *Grande Polonaise* in A-flat Major, Op. 53. After intermission Greenhouse and Pressler performed the *Allegro Spirituoso* by Senaillé, the *Valse Sentimentale* by Tchaikovsky, and the *Allegro Appassionato* by Saint Saëns.

Columbia Artists sent the Trio on the road in this fashion for years. Since chamber music was—for many of their audiences—hard to swallow, the Trio sweetened the pill. Pressler says, "It was like medicine which they say is good for you but you don't have to like it. So we played the solos to make them like it." He admits, sotto voce, to having edited some trios in order to make room for the fleshy, flashy middle. In 1958, they began with the Saint-Saëns Trio in F Major, Op. 18, and ended once again with Mendelssohn's Second Piano Trio. The solos were as follows: Guilet, with Pressler, performed Tartini and Kreisler's *Variations,* then Debussy and Hartmann's *The Girl with the Flaxen Hair,* then Bazzini's *Scherzo Fantastique.* Pressler played a scherzo in E Minor by Mendelssohn, Chopin's Nocturne in C-sharp Minor, Op. 27, No. 1 and Liszt's *Rakóczy March.* After intermission Pressler accompanied Greenhouse in Glazunov's *Serenade Espagnole,* Paradis's *Sicilienne,* and Popper's *Elfentanz.*

Thereafter they would add such pyrotechnics as Fiocco's *Allegro,* Sarasate's *Carmen Fantasy* on a theme by Bizet, Prokofiev's *Suggestions Diaboliques,* Op. 4, Liszt's version of Paganini's *The Little Bell,* Trowell's transcription of Francoeur's Sonata in E Major, and Granados's Intermezzo from *Goyescas.* As late as the 1968–69 season, the Community Concert Association flier presented Guilet and Pressler performing *Variations on a Theme of Corelli,* then Debussy's *En bateau* and Ravel's *Perpetuum Mobile.* Pressler's solo interlude consisted of Scriabin's Etude in D-sharp Minor, Op. 8, No. 12, Chopin's Nocturne, Op. 27, No. 2, and the Triana from *Iberia* by Albeniz. After intermission Greenhouse teamed with Pressler to provide Silot's rendering of Bach's Adagio from the Toccata, Adagio, and Fugue for Organ in C Major, and Chopin's *Introduction and Polonaise Brillante,* Op. 3.

Of community concerts, Pressler says, "They use you up and spit you out. For the young performer it can be very dangerous, it destroys both the body and soul." But in those years, indispensably, they had the chance to work. "We fought, we scratched, we created what was a trio out of three people." While the janitors set up chairs in the high-school gym, in the basement of town halls and churches, in motel rooms across America, in improvised greenrooms and dining rooms cleared for the concert, in a patron's guesthouse or Grange hall or synagogue, driving, discussing the music on buses and trains and planes, in truck stops and college cafeterias, the men became a unit—and the unit held.

Greenhouse did most of the driving. He went through cars at an impressive rate—black Buicks, dark blue Oldsmobiles, a gray Imperial. They would drive all night in order to save on the lodging expenses; they would sing and whistle ("*J'aime l'ail, j'aime l'ail . . .*") in order to keep each other awake: "Don't put me in the scenery!" They recollect this, now, with nostalgia for youth's energy—but shaking their heads at the strain. The physical assault on a performer's health should not be underestimated; endurance and good humor count in a career.

Greenhouse says, "We arrived for one performance in the Midwest—I probably shouldn't mention the town—and there was a spinet piano onstage. It was terribly out of tune, but in those days we were just starting and hoped to make a good impression. So Pressler began the concert on the spinet upright—and as he went along he became angrier and angrier. Finally he was so angry with the piano that he broke five or six strings. By the end of the concert we barely had enough strings to play . . ."

"Some page turners," Pressler says, "will read slower than I do, some will read faster. Some are critics—they turn the page, tsk-tsk. Some sing. Some other one, he's impatient, he'll look all the time at his watch. And some can't even read music. That's the worst."

There was a piano in which one midrange key failed to function. "Just don't use that note too often," the local sponsor advised. There was a concert in De Kalb, Illinois—for which the Beaux Arts had been announced as a string trio. "Consequently," Greenhouse remembers, "the superintendent of the building decided that we wouldn't need a piano. There was no piano onstage when we arrived; it was down in the pit. The superintendent said, 'It's too late to call the piano movers; how are we going to work this out?' He said, 'Why not adjust things so that the piano plays in the pit and the two strings play up onstage?' But Pressler objected to that very much. And then he suggested all three of us play in the pit. So the string players objected. We said we'd come back at a future date and redo the concert. But he said, 'No, there are twelve hundred people coming to hear the performance tonight, you can't disappoint them.' So we suggested he call for volunteers to lift the enormous nine-foot Steinway from the pit onto the stage. And about five minutes to eight he got up onstage and asked for volunteers. There were lots of young husky college students who came forward and lined up around the piano; then they counted off, one, two, three, lift! And they lifted the piano—it came up about four feet above the stage—and they dropped it! So all the pedals came off. And since there was no tuner, Menahem had to play without any pedals. We managed."

What they managed, over time and with tenacity, was to build an audience. Repeatedly, they had return engagements; increasingly, they gave concerts in major musical forums: at Hunter College, the Library of Congress, the Grace Rainey Rodgers Auditorium. A career extends between the young man's aspiration and the old man's achievement; to move from "promising" to "distinguished" takes decades. In 1964 a recording (of Dvořák and Mendelssohn) received the Grand Prix du Disque; in September 1983, and with reference to their entire discography, the Trio won the Prix d'Honneur du Prix Mondial. By now the literature has been established; an audience who arrived to hear the Beaux Arts Trio would be shocked by such programs as the potpourri above. In this regard the three musicians blazed a trail; they have rendered no small service to the young performer by simply staying on. A professional life as member of a piano trio is possible today in part because Guilet, Greenhouse, and Pressler demonstrated the plausibility thereof; it does not seem so wild a gamble now.

Young trios spring up hydra-headed these years. Many will disband from disappointment or pure weariness; arguments will split the personnel. Some will make careers as soloists, some will join an orchestra or play in pickup bands. Some will enter medical school or the foreign service or the advertising industry and quit. But somewhere out there, surely, is that group which will be hailed as heir apparent to the Beaux Arts Trio (". . . worthy successors to the last great trio . . .") as they themselves were hailed, in 1955, by Charles Munch.

Pressler wrote an article, "Why Play Chamber Music?" for an as-yet-unpublished volume on chamber music by the C. F. Peters Corporation. It is brief, addressed to the young performer, and offers "the thesis that chamber music should be an indispensable part of the training of any serious musician." He stresses "three aspects of playing chamber music which are, in my opinion, of the greatest benefit to the practitioner. These are: hearing, balance, and ensemble." His thoughts on these three matters are worth quoting in entirety:

> *Hearing.* Since the substance of music is sound, a musician must forever keep developing his physical ear and his imaginative sense of sound, or inner ear. When a musician practices his instrument alone there is only one consciousness at work: the same mind produces the sounds and judges their quality. Needless to say, we are all constrained by our natural limitations and biases; habit, too, can dull the edge of our auditory acuity, especially when it comes to our own playing. On the other hand, when playing, and especially when rehearsing chamber music one must listen keenly not only to one's own sound but to that of one's partners. Moreover, one's partners are not only different musical personalities with their own particular abilities, but often play different instruments with different sound characteristics. This in itself

already expands enormously the realm of sound of which the player is made constantly aware, and which he must absorb and assimilate. However, this is only the beginning, for the chamber musician has the task of doing his part in blending these diverse sounds into a cohesive and seamless entity. For this he must develop a whole range of sounds in order either to match the sounds of others by imitation, or to enhance them by creating a contrasting sound, or to bring them out by giving them the correct support, or even to cover up a weakness of another player. Similarly, one is the object of the critical scrutiny of one's co-players who can come up with comments, suggestions, or demands that spur a search for new tonal possibilities and a continuous refinement and enrichment of the range of sonorities at one's command.

Balance. If sound is the exclusive domain of the musician, balance is one of the cardinal principles of all art forms, and it is balance which contributes, perhaps more than any other element, to the sense of perfection of a work of art. Unfortunately, its difficulty is commensurate with its importance. Although a sense of balance is to some extent intuitive, it is also the result of tireless experimentation. What was said before about sound applies equally to dynamics, phrasing, color, tempo, voicing, and all the other elements that have to be balanced in a musical performance. Unlike playing in the orchestra, where the conductor alone determines the balance, in chamber music every player is personally responsible for the balance and contributes to shaping it. At the other end of the spectrum is the soloist who is completely free and independent of others, but not of the inexorable exigencies of balance. It is the experience of playing in a chamber music group, more than any other, that cultivates and heightens any musician's sense of balance which is as subtle and as tricky for the soloist as it is for the chamber music player, or the conductor. Chamber music is truly ideal for this purpose because it is midway—in complexity and in the amount of freedom that it gives—between the orchestra and solo work. We must be grateful, therefore, that this unsurpassed medium for forging and honing one's sense of balance is now so easily available.

Ensemble. Most of us who are students are musically almost completely dependent on our teachers. We endeavour to follow faithfully whatever our teachers tell us to do, and our sense of musical "rightness" depends largely on their approval. Those of us who are solo performers run the real risk of becoming idiosyncratic and mannered, while those of us who teach, working with individuals far less advanced than ourselves, may tend to become dogmatic. Being regularly active in a chamber music group can be an antidote to all these threatening excesses, whether they be an excess of timidity, of self-centeredness, or of intolerance to disagreement. In chamber music we unite in ourselves all three roles. We have to lead and to follow, we play our solos and we accompany. We teach and learn from each other. We fight for the acceptance of our musical ideas, but we also learn to listen to and appreciate the ideas of others, and we yield when need be. We must always try to keep an open mind and a sincere willingness to try out new ideas. When passions run high, we have to mediate and referee, as well as to cool off and compromise. We do all of this so that the end product will be a true ensemble in which the whole is much greater than the sum of the individual parts.

It is obvious that there can be no polish without abrasion. Furthermore, the higher the polish the more scraping and the more friction it takes. Naturally, musical performances are no exception. A chamber music group can approach perfection of ensemble only by going through this grueling grind. But in the process nerves also can become frayed and egos bruised. This is a real danger. More than one outstanding and successful chamber music group broke up under the overwhelming pressure created by the conflict between the dictates of a perfect ensemble—the absolute integration of all the players—and the human frailties of ego rebellion and worn-out nerves. . . .

Columbia Artists Management was and remains instrumental in the group's success. The Trio have been represented by that organization since they began; after Arthur Judson, they came under the "personal direction" of Michael Ries and, since Ries's death in 1983, David Foster. The crucial witness to their workaday world is, however, Hattie Clark. If Casadesus provided the musical imprimatur for the Beaux Arts Trio, Hattie Clark provides the glue. Her office in the CAMI Building on West Fifty-seventh Street is clogged with memorabilia, her desk piled high with call-back slips and contracts and memos and snapshots of grandchildren and record albums and brochures. She writes the approach and confirmation letters and sends out publicity and Christmas gifts and clears the concerts with each of the three men—a daunting task, since they have additional commitments and can be hard to reach. The Trio agree with CAMI to give over blocks of time to concert tours in North and South America as well as the Far East; they have separate managements in Europe.

Then Hattie Clark—a diminutive, bright-eyed person of unflagging energy—fills in the dates. For the Trio nowadays this task is largely custodial; early on, however, it took promotional zeal. (She has other groups also, of course. The CAMI brochure for 1983–84 lists the following instrumental ensembles: Beaux Arts Trio, Boston Symphony Chamber Players, Chamber Music Society of Lincoln Center, Music from Marlboro, New York Renaissance Band, Panocha String Quartet, Amati String Quartet, Orlando String Quartet, Empire Brass Quintet, Romeros Quartet, Romeros Trio, Aspen Soloists, Canterbury Trio, Pacific Soloists, Toccata and Flourishes, David Golub, Mark Kaplan, Colin Carr Trio, Harvey Pittel Saxophone Quartet, and Aurora Trio.) The "contract slips" provide the requisite data for a performance and, taken in conjunction, make up a kind of itinerary for a concert tour.

Take one example: the South Mountain concerts. The Trio have been playing at South Mountain (in Pittsfield, Massachusetts, just north of Tanglewood) for nearly thirty years. The concert hall itself is a barn; it seats six hundred people. The series is sold out routinely, and to "regulars" who bring picnics to the meadow by the barn. Mrs. Willem Willeke—Sally—is an old friend, and the musicians could find "the presentor" with no trouble. But the contract slip (dated February 26, for a performance on Sunday, September 27, at 3:00 P.M.) provides them with Mrs. Willeke's business and home phone and address, reminds them that she will have furnished a Steinway concert grand, that they are to meet and rehearse "anytime before the concert," and gives them their hotel. It states the agreed-on compensation and the unvarying 20 percent thereof that is CAMI's commission. For Osaka, Taipei, or Santiago, the slips are similar. Each musician carries a date book and—as tour-time approaches—receives a detailed itinerary from CAMI's travel agent; like all who must travel to work, the Trio are creatures of airports and rented cars and beds. A season extends from September 1 of one year through August 31 of the ensuing one; the Trio know where they should be a minimum of one year in advance.

"Chamber Music," according to *Grove's Dictionary,* "is the name applied to all that class of music which is specially fitted for performance in a room, as distinguished from concert music, or dramatic music, or ecclesiastical music, of such other kinds as require many performers and large spaces for large volumes of sound."

This is an inclusive definition, and there are many kinds of chamber music, many rooms. The earliest widespread usage of the term *musica da camera* appeared in Italy in the latter part of the sixteenth century. There was no sharp differentiation between vocal and instrumental music, and the first publication to which the English term was applied—Martin Peerson's *Mottects or Grave Chamber Music* (1630)—consisted of "Songs of five parts . . . fit for Voyces and Vials, with an Organ Part." The "sonatas" of the early seventeenth century were in part modeled on and closely related to vocal techniques, and the collection of dance tunes, or suites, could be performed by various combinations of instruments. The "sound piece"—sonata—was popularized by the clavier, and the development of violin technique gave rise to the duet sonata; with the addition of the bass, the trio sonata became the most important type of baroque chamber music. By the middle of the eighteenth century, and principally in Haydn's hands, the quartet for solo strings emerged as the popular form; it takes pride of place in "classical" chamber music. The piano trio derived essentially from the keyboard sonatas, with *ad libitum* parts for violin and violoncello, and there was a marked domination, in Haydn, of the piano part. Mozart liberated the strings, to a degree, from their subordinate role—and that process was continued and made complete by Beethoven.

The literature is rich. Brahms, Schubert, and Schumann (to add three names to those already noted) composed acknowledged masterworks for this combination of instruments. Dvořák, Fauré, Mendelssohn, and Tchaikovsky belong in the long list. The Beaux Arts Trio include twentieth-century music in their repertoire—works by David Baker, Aaron Copland, Ingolf Dahl, John Eaton, Wolfgang Fortner, Bernhard Heiden, and Vittorio Rieti, for example. They play the Ives, Ravel, and Shostakovitch Trios with some frequency. Yet the vast majority of their concert and recording material antedates the present century; the Beaux Arts do not feel at ease with "modern" music. (This is rather more true of Greenhouse and Pressler than of Cohen, who does attempt to stay abreast of contemporary techniques.) The men can sight-read Haydn, whereas they would have to spend weeks of rehearsal time in order to acquire a "new" piece. When Greenhouse premiered the Elliot Carter Sonata, "It took me forever to learn. Now," he says, "my students play it with no trouble. It's almost as if you have to be born into the period. . . ."

The amateur or professional musician can make a lifetime of music within the repertoire. The amateur, indeed, is more likely to play chamber music than the solo literature for his instrument—though he will practice the latter. And the organizational commitment for orchestral work looms large; community orchestras, if not few, are far between. Three of four friends, or members of a family, can meet together weekly as a chamber music group; "all that class of music which is specially fitted for performance in a room" permits the devotee to play at home and needs no rented space.

This has had its consequences for the Beaux Arts Trio. Chamber music, almost by definition, has attracted a smaller audience than those who follow soloists or flock to Symphony Hall. It is an intimate form. The musicians face each other, or used to, and placement is an issue; it would be inappropriate if all four members of a string quartet regarded only the audience, projecting out at "the fourth wall." A group may have a leader but not a conductor; the literature concerns itself with balance and responsiveness. Chamber music, as the name implies (Joyce made a bathroom joke of it), is art "in camera."

Further, the primacy of solo performance is deeply embedded in Western cultural attitudes. The history of virtuoso recitals is in fact quite recent; only with Liszt and Paganini do we find the spectacle of a single named artist on tour. But the arithmetic of attention-getting verges on the geometric; we think of a single performer as twice as important as two, four times as important as each member of a quartet, and so on down the line. There is an inverse proportion to fame: the members of a consort are virtually nameless, and an orchestra's collective face has faceless component parts. The players are "first horn" or "second chair," not "Mr. A——," "Ms. B——." The interpretative artist who plays chamber music—no matter how successful—subordinates himself to the idea of an ensemble; there will be fifty folk who have heard of (and have attended concerts and purchased the recordings of) the Amadeus or Budapest or Guarneri or Juilliard quartets for every one who can tell you their violists' names.

There have been, until recently, two conventional wisdoms as to chamber music. They are opposed and foolish, but widespread. The first is that the chamber musician, for reasons adduced above, is less accomplished and important than the soloist. The second is that chamber music groups can be composed of soloists on their days off. Since a piano trio breaks down into component parts more readily than a quintet or octet, such attitudes are manifested more frequently about its personnel: put three virtuosi in a room, give them a day to rehearse, and out comes a performance. Pressler is vehement about this. "Truly a trio it isn't," he says, when asked about such great exemplars as Cortot, Casals, and Thibaud, or Rubinstein, Piatigorsky, and Heifetz. He admires them as virtuosi—"Just to hear them tune would have been sufficient!"—but insists on the ongoing demands of ensemble. "What you hear are three splendid fellows," he says. "You don't hear Schubert or Brahms."

Eugene Istomin, Isaac Stern, and Leonard Rose provide a contemporary instance of soloists who play together as a piano trio; their every appearance is an occasion, and they can fill Carnegie Hall. There are other notable groupings. But the Beaux Arts Trio are, to my knowledge, the professional piano trio with the longest record of ensemble performance in history. That record of longevity will not be challenged soon. Rounded off, the Trio have performed for thirty years at an average of one hundred concerts per year. (In the beginning they performed fewer than one hundred dates each season; now they perform rather more.) And three thousand concerts, approximately, are thousands more than any other piano trio have ever undertaken—or are likely to for decades. A sufficient change in quantity brings qualitative change. The five hundredth time one addresses Ravel must be different than the fifth.

Longevity has its risks, of course—staleness and inattention principal among them. The Beaux Arts have their off nights, their automatic performances. The drive for personal primacy is not always under control. But they have set the standard against which other ensembles will be measured; they have established, beyond all dispute, that a piano trio can both survive and succeed. It is worth repeating that such an argument was made long since for the string quartet. But the piano trio—with its opposition between keyboard and strings—seems less of a matched ensemble, more easily disjoined.

That is no longer the case. Pressler says, "It has to be one spirit, one ideal. Everybody plays everybody else's note, in the true sense." In an interview as "Musicians of the Month" for *Musical America* (the cover story, April 1978), they address the matter of balance.

> Cohen says, "In a quartet the players can adjust to one another. In a trio, the conviction lies with the piano; if anything goes wrong it is the string player who is 'out.'"
>
> Greenhouse touched on a key issue. "Of necessity, we have to use tempered intonation, whereas a quartet is freer to use intonation for expressive purposes."
>
> "The lower the piano goes," Cohen added, "the sharper the pitch becomes, and the higher it goes, the flatter. So the strings tend to be flat to the piano in

the low register and sharp in the high register. When Bernie and I play with the piano in the bass we get as high as our ear will let us, without playing actually out of tune."

"One really winces, going down," said Pressler. "There's an E-flat arpeggio in Beethoven's Opus 11 . . ."

"By the time he gets to that last note," laughed Cohen. "He's so far *off*!"

Charles Rosen, in *The Classical Style*, addresses the problem succinctly.

> Instrumental changes since the eighteenth century have made a problem out of the balance of sound in Haydn's piano trios, and, in fact, in all chamber music with piano. Violin necks (including, of course, even those of all the Stradivariuses and Guarneris) have been lengthened, making the strings tauter: the bows are used today with hairs considerably more tight as well. The sound is a good deal more brilliant, fatter and more penetrating. A less selective use of vibrato has added to the contrast. The piano, in turn, has become louder, richer, even mushier in sound, and, above all, less wiry and metallic. . . . Both the piano and the violin are now louder, but the piano is less piercing, the violin more. Violinists today have to make an effort of self-sacrifice to allow the piano to sing out softly; to do so is as much an exercise in virtue as in musicianship.

And this brings us full circle to the original decision to employ no surnames in the title "The Beaux Arts Trio of

New York." Theirs is a collective enterprise, their tradition that of an ensemble. They moved with only a hitch in their stride through the shift of personnel—when Guilet retired at seventy and Cohen came in. Greenhouse nears seventy now, and the others are past sixty; there will come a time when the present performers retire.

A large and growing audience, however, will remain. Recently the Beaux Arts have been called: "The leading piano trio in the world today" *(The New York Times)*; "The touchstone of excellence in this most intimate of music making" *(Gramophone)*; and "One of chamber music's handful of supergroups" *(The Los Angeles Times)*. *Time* magazine affirmed, "Among the world's piano trios there is none better," and there are no higher honors in the recording industry than those they have received. But their ongoing legacy is to have made legitimate the piano trio as ensemble for a musician's career.

Chapter Two

Bernard Greenhouse gave his first concert as a boy soprano with the Crusade Union Boy Singers; the group toured the American South. He then played dinner music for fifty cents an hour at the Pine Tree Inn in Lakehurst, New Jersey. During the Second World War—and sounding, by his own testimonial, "like Donald Duck"—he played oboe for the United States Navy Band. Since childhood, however, his chosen instrument has been the cello; he has been a concert performer all his adult life. He has had a career as soloist, as a member of the Bach Aria Group, and with various short-term ensembles; he is a founding member of the Beaux Arts Trio. Mr. Greenhouse teaches at the Manhattan School of Music and New York State University at Stony Brook; he has taught at Hartford University in Connecticut, Indiana University at Bloomington, the Juilliard School, and elsewhere; he plays the "Paganini," ex-"Countess of Stanlein" Stradivarius of 1707.

Greenhouse was born on January 1, 1916, in Newark, New Jersey; he is married to the former Aurora Menendez. He has two daughters, Nancy and Elena; he divides his "at home" time between Argyle, a small farming town in upstate New York, the village of Poquott on Long Island, and Wellfleet, Massachusetts. The following interview was conducted over a three-day period at his home on Cape Cod; it fell naturally if loosely into three parts. First we discussed his experiences as a student, then the career of the concert performer, and then the experience of teaching. Those days would have been pleasant, I believe, for any interviewer; Greenhouse is as gracious as he is informed. But they were made the more rewarding, for me, in that an articulate artist talked at length about matters on which he is by habit reticent. My questions are signaled by the abbreviation for Interviewer, "Int.," his answers by the initials "B.G."

Int.: Before you became a performer and teacher you were, of course, a student. Could you describe some of the men that you worked with, and their approach to teaching?

B.G.: I studied with Felix Salmond at the Juilliard. He was very exacting as to the score and sources of the work we had before us. He was an artist to the core, and he insisted on the beauty of performance—but his teaching was not particularly inclusive as far as technique was concerned. He was not a gifted technician. I don't believe he was terribly interested in contemporary music; his interest did not go into the realm of, for instance, Stravinsky. He was enormously exciting as a musician, yet his choice of music was always on the classic side.

On the other hand, the greatest cellist of the time was Emanuel Feuermann. I had the good fortune to work with him for a period which extended over two years—and that was a very different proposition. He insisted on five or six hours of hard technical labor every day; he was a sarcastic man, and his lessons were a terror. He could be enormously caustic. His response to my lessons was always the same; he would say to me, "If you practice very hard, six, eight hours a day, someday you may be able to make a living out of your cello." But, on the other hand, things would come back to me which he would say to other musicians; apparently he praised me to the skies. He was very fond of my talent—but never to my face, he was never encouraging to me.

I remember once becoming very excited about doing a debut recital at Town Hall. And I thought, well, I'd better get the advice of Mr. Feuermann. So I rushed up to Scarsdale where he was living, and with great enthusiasm I broached the fact that I wanted to play this recital at Town Hall. "What do you want to do that for?" he said. "I'm one of the best-known cellists in the country. I have only twelve engagements for next year so far. The cello is not an instrument which is going to bring you success, so why don't you just skip it and forget about your plan?" I remember leaving completely crestfallen. It actually took another six or eight years before I made my debut—and that was after Feuermann had died.

Int.: With whom were you working by then?

B.G.: While I was in the navy, I had a weekend pass to come to New York. And on the train I met Mischa Schneider—the cellist of the Budapest Quartet—who was on his way to a coaching session with Diran Alexanian. We had a long discussion about Alexanian; Mischa was tremendously impressed, and he invited me to come along and hear the lesson. They were working on a Bach suite. I was thrilled—so enormously excited about his musical gifts that I too started coaching with Alexanian. As we became more and more friendly, I discovered that there were great discrepancies—not in musical taste, but in the techniques of playing the instrument. His approach was one of great stiffness. His hands were tense; it was forced—it was the kind of work which required enormous numbers of hours, of extensions, and the bow arm was quite tight. We got into lengthy arguments about technique—the way in which relaxation can be achieved in both the left and right hands. He allowed me to argue; it was usually after I had played for him. I would play for an hour or so, and he would make musical suggestions, and then we would go off to dinner together and continue the discussions on a technical basis. That's where we got into very great differences of opinion—not in an angry manner, but by comparing notes.

Int.: You used two terms just now: teaching session and coaching session. Are they interchangeable or would a coaching session come when a cellist has demonstrated a certain degree of prowess on his own?

B.G.: A coaching session could be carried out even between two colleagues. If you wanted the opinion of a colleague, and were able to take it—if you respected him enough to follow his advice, then it would be a coaching session. A teaching session is where the student will arrive and listen to everything the teacher has to say. He must try, at least for a short time, to produce everything the teacher advises; he must follow that teacher's advice to the letter. He can change only after he's stopped studying with the particular teacher. So there is a substantial distinction. In a coaching session, two people arrive at some sort of conclusion together.

I should add here that Alexanian helped me to meet with Casals. I had traveled quite a bit as soloist by that time, and had had a series of concerts in New York. But Alexanian felt it would be very useful for me to study with Casals. So he wrote a letter on my behalf, but Casals was, as you know, very much occupied with the Spanish Republican cause at that point.

Int.: In 1946?

B.G.: Correct. We had a lengthy correspondence, and he refused to teach me. But I did not accept the negative reply. So I took a troop transport right after the war—after I'd come out of the navy. I enrolled in the American School at Fontainebleau as a means to get a visa.

Int.: Carrying your cello with you, or a suitcase?

B.G.: Both. I had several cases with all sorts of food which I knew would be in short supply—baking chocolate, tinned butter, that sort of thing. After I arrived in Paris, I wrote another, final postcard asking whether he wouldn't hear me play just once. And I received a card in Paris, saying that if I came on such and such a date, he would be pleased to hear me play—providing I would give a check to Spanish Republican charities. When I received the card I was, of course, overjoyed. I made arrangements to take the train to Perpignan and then the mountain railway up to Prades. And I arrived at the railway station speaking barely a word of French. There was someone with a handdrawn cart who took my valise; I carried the cello. We went down the main street into Prades to the Grand Hotel. But the owner of the note shook his finger at me and said—the porter translating—"No more cellists can come to my hotel. I already had one. Casals. He disturbed all the guests."

So I had to wend my way over to the midwife's. She happened to have a room free at the time, a room just barely wide enough for the bed—with no possibility of practicing. The same day I went to the Villa Colette and knocked on Casals's door. I was let in. Within minutes Casals came down from his studio, still in his pajamas; he had been writing letters. And he said, "You have come a long way and been very persistent. Why have you come here to study with me?" We sat down, had a long discussion. I gave him my background and told him some of the works which I had performed; I said he had been my idol ever since I was ten. He said, "You go back to your room and come back in two days in the morning, and I will hear you play."

Well, the next days were anxious ones for me. . . . I went back on the appointed morning, entered the room, and Casals still hadn't dressed. He was still in his pajamas. He said, "Well, now you warm up, play a bit so that you get your hands in good condition and I will be back as soon as I have dressed and shaved." I took the cello out of the case and worked for twenty minutes or so, and there was no Casals. I had had my back turned to the door, and when finally I turned I could see his bald head in the doorway—he had been listening at the keyhole. When he saw that I had turned my head, he came into the room, still in his pajamas, still unshaven, and he said, "I really didn't want to dress. I wanted to hear you without having you nervous."

Then he started asking for the repertoire, and he requested many pieces. After an hour or more of my playing—during which he indicated nothing more than the piece and the passage he wanted me to play—he said, "All right. Put down your cello, put it away, and we'll talk." And I thought, now here comes the worthwhile contribution to a Republican charity. But he said to me, "Well. What you need is an apprenticeship to a great artist. I believe in the apprentice system. Stradivarius, Guarnerius, Amati—they turned out so many wonderful violin makers. And I believe the same thing can hold true in making musicians. If I knew of a great artist I could send you to, I would do so," he said, "because my mind is occupied with the Spanish Republican cause. But since I don't know whom to send you to—and if you agree to stay in the village and take a lesson at least once every two days—I will teach you."

So I went to Paris for my trunks, came back, and settled in. At this point the gentleman who owned the Grand Hotel—when he found out that I had chocolate and good American dollars—changed his mind about having a cellist in residence. So I moved into the Grand Hotel, had a palatial room with a view, and from that point on I started to work very hard. I had three or four lessons a week.

Int.: With the proceeds going to the Spanish Republican cause?

B.G.: When I asked Casals how much he would charge a lesson, he said twenty dollars. In those days such a sum was considerable. But one day I arrived in great spirits and I played a beautiful performance—forgive me, I think it *was* beautiful—of the Brahms F Major Sonata. And when I finished he said, "You know, you played so well today I won't accept the twenty dollars." And I was deliriously happy. But the next lesson, unfortunately, I didn't play so well, and he accepted the twenty dollars. This went on for a week or two until finally he said to me, "You know, I can't accept this money from you; I know it's going to be difficult. But someday when you're able to, I would like you to write a check for Spanish Republican charities and make a considerable contribution." And I agreed; this is a promise I've kept. But from that point on the lessons were free—astonishing.

Int.: What other kinds of pedagogical strategies did he have—other than listening behind a closed door?

B.G.: We spent at least three hours a lesson. The first hour was performance; the next hour entailed discussion of musical techniques; and the third hour he reminisced about his own career. During the first hour, he sat about a yard away. He would play a phrase and have me repeat it. And if the bowing and the fingering weren't exactly the same as his, and the emphasis on the top of the phrase was not the same, he would stop me and say, "No, no. Do it this way." And this went on for quite a few lessons. I was studying the Bach D Minor Suite and he demanded that I become an absolute copy. At one point I did very gingerly suggest that I would only turn out to be a poor copy of Pablo Casals, and he said to me, "Don't worry about that. Because I'm seventy years old, and I will be gone soon, and people won't remember my playing but they will hear yours." It turned out of course that he lived till the ripe old age of ninety-seven. But that was his way of teaching.

Int.: Was he very insistent about it?

B.G.: Yes. He was extremely meticulous about my following all the details of his performance. And after several weeks of working on that one suite of Bach's, finally, the two of us could sit down and perform and play all the same fingerings and bowings and all of the phrasings alike. And I really had become a copy of the Master. It was as if that room had stereophonic sound—two cellos producing at once. And at that point, when I had been able to accomplish this, he said to me, "Fine. Now just sit. Put your cello down and listen to the D Minor Suite." And he played through the piece and changed *every* bowing and *every* fingering and *every* phrasing and all the emphasis within the phrase. I sat there, absolutely with my mouth open, listening to a performance which was heavenly, absolutely beautiful. And when he finished he turned to me with a broad grin on his face, and he said, "Now you've learned how to improvise in Bach. From now on you study Bach this way."

Int.: So he was more a teacher than a coach?

B.G.: Assuredly. But I don't think Casals was very much interested in the techniques—not in the end. Yet he made many suggestions which were pertinent to and influential in my changing aspects of sound. For instance, he was most careful about vibrato. He said, "You know, you're very gifted, but there's a slight vulgarity to your playing, and it's because you do not use the vibrato to make music. You have an automatic motion to your left hand, which means that there is no help to the bow arm in what you do."

It meant that I had to change my whole left-hand technique. He sent me back to my studio to work without any vibrato at all. "Come back next lesson without any vibrato. But I want a musical performance in spite of the lack." Well, I found that enormously difficult to do—because my hand had become accustomed to constant motion. At length I was able to satisfy him.

Then we started producing vibrato in several different manners, using different parts of the arm. One was an arm vibrato for the lower strings; another was an elbow vibrato for the middle strings; a finger vibrato for the upper, higher register. This ability to vary the speed and the width of the vibrato changed my whole approach to phrasing. It was like a whole new spectrum—instead of having just the three primary colors, or perhaps one of the primary colors, you have the entire spectrum. And that has changed my whole approach. This all comes, as I said, from an issue of pure technique—but its implications are far more than technical.

Int.: Could you talk briefly about the distinction in terms of a career between solo performance and chamber music?

B.G.: I started out as a soloist. I was determined to play only solo concerts, but I found it an enormous strain. There are many facets to a talent. In order to be a great soloist, you must not only be able to perform well on the instrument but must also, for instance, have great confidence as far as memory is concerned. Rostropovitch has this confidence; he can study a score and memorize it quickly and be certain when he walks on stage that the whole thing's in his head. You must have the desire to sit in front of an audience alone; you must be hungry for success, must want it desperately. There are so many facets of talent and desire; if one of them is missing you will not enjoy a career.

So in spite of the fact that I had had moderate

success as soloist, it took more out of me than I felt able to expend. I felt terribly depressed because I searched for a perfection that I never reached. Even a single note out of place would disturb me; the preparation for those concerts provoked much anxiety. At one point I decided that I wanted to enjoy my music making and have a little less responsibility. And when I was asked whether I would consider forming the Beaux Arts Trio—well, it wasn't formal at that point, it was two friends who wanted to play a few trio concerts—I accepted. Pressler, Guilet, and I agreed to play eight or ten concerts the first season. But the engagements came in so quickly that the first season we had eighty concerts instead of eight. I enjoyed making music with my two friends, and I thought, what a wonderful way to spend one's life! And as a steady diet I prefer the chamber music world, with its varied repertoire, to the rather desolate career of traveling alone and the responsibilities involved.

Int.: Would you say that this variety in performance is an intrinsic and necessary part of an ongoing relation to the instrument, or are there certain definitive performances? A recording does not alter when you hear it fifty times. How do you feel about going into a recording studio as opposed to the stage?

B.G.: I approach the recording studio exactly the same way that I approach a concert performance. The difference is that in a concert performance the small inaccuracies go by. On a recording, if there are small inaccuracies, you have the opportunity to redo sections. But the inspiration is yours whether you're in front of an audience or a microphone; you must *ex-*

press something. You know that it's going to be played eventually for an audience, so that your reaction is the same. There's a little bit of tension in recording, a little bit more than you would have in a concert hall, because you might have an inspired moment but then a small blemish which negates the performance. You must look for that inspiration again. Now if that goes on several times, you have the blemish along with the inspiration, and finally you lose the latter because you're much more concerned with the blemish than with the inspiration. I have spent uncounted hours in recording studios. There are times when the work, the performance, goes very quickly and easily, and there are other times when it's a total waste. Fortunately we have a fine recording company—Philips—and they don't stint on time. We can walk into a studio at ten o'clock in the morning and decide an hour later that we're not going to get anyplace and come back at midnight to do the recording.

Int.: What are some of the dynamics of performing in a chamber music ensemble? Has it ever happened to you that you've been surprised onstage by a sudden variation in a performance—by something unexpected on your colleague's part?

B.G.: Generally, the excitement of performance comes when you can judge what your colleague is going to do at the moment he decides to do it. I don't mean by this that the performance should ever be according to rote. We attempt to keep a feeling of improvisation and to avoid the automatic; we search for that, always, in rehearsal and through instantaneous changes onstage. We search for freshness of approach to the old works as well as to newer contemporary work. It's a problem when you've had a group playing together for years. Take the Ravel Trio. We've given perhaps a thousand performances of the Ravel, and yet we have to keep the freshness of presentation. The one way to do that is through rehearsal—searching for new ways to interpret the piece.

Int.: You have said that you hear a phrase in your head before you transfer it to the instrument. Is that also true of your colleagues—can you predict their intonation?

B.G.: Yes. The intonation in the case of the piano, of course, depends on the piano tuner—and that can be a great problem. But Isidore Cohen replaced Daniel Guilet a long time ago as the violinist in this trio. And I feel—surely this is reciprocal—that I have learned to know his intonation to the point where I adjust to it. There are many ways of expressing intonation. There is what we call expressive intonation, which has nothing to do with the tempered scale of the piano. When one plays in conjunction with the piano, of course, one must use this expressive intonation a little less frequently. There is something to be gained, however, through the use of expressive intonation: a scale which is perhaps a little bit on the lower side will give a feeling of sorrow more than a tempered scale. So we adjust intonation to the point where we create the particular mood. In a light Mendelssohn scherzo, for instance, we will attempt to play a little on the higher side to convey his sense of joy.

Int.: I think it's fair to say—and correct me if it isn't—that the world of chamber music has expanded in the last few years. The audience is growing, and seems both more enthusiastic and learned. A decade ago, however, conventional wisdom had it that the world of chamber music would and must contract because its appreciative audience was of an elder generation. Yet the great chamber ensembles seem as prominent as solo performers nowadays. Does this surprise you?

B.G.: It's a bit of a shock, actually, because we now appear very often to young audiences or in a university context. They are knowledgeable and committed students of classical music, and they come of course not only to our concerts but to those of other groups. It shouldn't be surprising, however, because the effort of three or four people working together is something magnificent. When you have an integration of instruments working as a unity, it is something which people admire. There's so little of that in this world. There's so little which people can admire in the general ensemble of four or four thousand human beings.

And then, of course, you have the repertoire itself. I think the masters put their great effort, their best creative energies into chamber music. You will not find in the symphonic works of Schubert anything to equal the Schubert C Major Quintet. Brahms did some of his great writing in the chamber literature. Beethoven—how can anyone compare the late string quartets with, for instance, his earlier works for orchestra? And therefore I think people have come to realize that the world of chamber music presents something unusual—a collaboration in the broadest sense between the composer and the performing artists, a group that must be and function as one.

Int.: Implicit in all you've been saying is a double assertion as to craft as a lonely business—hours by yourself practicing—and the sense of a shared enterprise. And implicit in this statement is a question: do you have a sense of community as you travel, even though you're in a new town or country every second night?

B.G.: There are a large number of cities which are no longer new to us. We have done at least a hundred performances in New York, for example, so we have an audience there. And one can look out into the audience for a moment before starting to play and recognize people because they take the same seats in the auditorium. They come year after year; they are our friends even though we have never met them personally.

And the audience, too, travels. We might give a concert in Vancouver and then at the Bath Festival in England and meet someone who comes backstage to say, well, I heard you in Vancouver; when do you plan to return?

Int.: What of your own instrument? You mentioned that you're somewhat at the mercy of a piano tuner with a piano—and there are virtuosi who bring both along on tour. Michelangeli, I'm told, travels with two pianos and a tuner in a truck.

B.G.: Yes, so he can discard one. . . . I too have trouble traveling. When they started charging full-fare tickets for the cello, I resented that a great deal. I would try to hide the fact that I had a cello by wrapping Menahem and Daniel around it when we went through airport gates. But that didn't work for very long. So I tried hoping I could get by with purchasing a half-price ticket for the instrument. On one occasion I walked up to a ticket agent, who looked at the half-price ticket and said, "How old is your child Cello, Mr. Greenhouse?" I told him—that was 1971—it was 264 years old. A friend of mine calls her cello a "bass balalaika" because there are no fare regulations covering the cost of shipment for a balalaika. Now I send the instrument first-class because they require broad seats for it—but they're generous enough to send me the caviar and complimentary drinks back through the curtain. I travel economy-class while the Strad sprawls grandly up front.

Int.: What variables pertain to a string instrument—your own?

B.G.: I believe that it need not be pampered. With today's travel we'll hop from a tropical climate to a cold country; the enormous changes in humidity and temperature with a new instrument would normally affect its playing quality. But in the case of the Strad I haven't found it difficult to make an adjustment. It has great sensitivity; it is like the human voice. And humidity will of course affect the sound. So one must allow the instrument to spring back to its best voice, and not to force adjustments because one day or week it's not at its best sounding.

This cello is one of the great works of Stradivarius. He made originally about sixty celli; he made many more violins—altogether I believe he might have made nine hundred instruments. There were only about fifteen violas, sixty celli, and the rest were violins. I think he made two guitars. Of the celli, fifteen remain in the original state, and no more than half are in private hands. I firmly believe that these are instruments to be performed on; they were not intended for museums or to be sequestered in glass cases.

Int.: These instruments, however, do tend to be sequestered. How can you avoid that, given their value?

B.G.: They have always had a value beyond price. I very often simply set the instrument in a corner of the room so that I can look at the beauty of the lines, of the carving, of the magnificent varnish. It has that beauty as well as the beauty of sound—a doubled value, if you wish. The acoustical marvels which Stradivarius achieved on these instruments are intrinsic and cannot be realized in a museum. All instruments in museums will deteriorate unless performed on.

Int.: It is sometimes difficult to determine from the stage how good the acoustics are in a given concert hall. Can something that seems very large from the performer's vantage be deadened by the tenth row—and vice versa?

B.G.: Yes. There's a discrepancy of perception. Very often we will come offstage, having been disappointed in the sound produced, and, as far as the audience is concerned, the sound is excellent. The acoustics have been fine for them. There are the "one-way" auditoriums, where the instruments sound good to the public but deadened to us. So we feel there's been a lack of enthusiasm, a lack of brio in the sound—but the reverse has been the case.

Int.: This leads to another kind of question, though it's related. How do you feel about critics? You've admitted that the reaction of other performers is important to you. And you've mentioned audience response—but what of those members of the audience who get complimentary seats?

B.G.: They are vital, of course, to anyone desiring a career. One cannot fight the opinion of a critic. Whether he's knowledgeable or not, his printed word has an enormous effect. Yet that doesn't mean that a group that has been before the public for decades cannot withstand a few acid remarks and poor reviews. And in this regard also, one never knows in advance. We've come offstage thinking one thing about our performance and are used to reading something very different about it next day. Very often a concert has had enormous success—with sustained applause after the program, much enthusiasm. But this will rile the critic, who wants to prove that he knows better than the audience. And, to the contrary, we will come offstage feeling very bad after a performance, feeling that the concert was a failure. But the next day's review will be sunshine. So there's no way for a performer to know the reaction of the critic; he can know the reaction of an audience because he can gauge it directly.

Int.: Have you ever read a piece of criticism that has altered your playing?

B.G.: It would be absolutely untrue to suggest that it does not affect us—at least for a few hours. I think it's forgotten very quickly, however. Just as yesterday's newspaper is stale news, so the critic's review becomes stale after a day or two. If he says that the balance is off or the intonation has suffered or there have been wrong notes, it will affect us for the next performance. But rarely beyond that. After twenty-five years, after having studied the works which we perform continually, the slightest nuance—the slightest change of tempo—has been studied and planned out. How can we expect to listen to a critic who attends *one* performance, and even though he might have it in front of him, doesn't really know the score? The only thing he can do is follow to see if we are carrying out the metronome markings, and then he would have to have a metronome along. By looking at the score, and perhaps having heard it four or five times in his life, how can he be expected to criticize a group which has performed and studied these works endlessly? We feel much more secure in our knowledge than he can possibly feel in his.

Int.: Now that the role is reversed—now that you are the recognized performer and students come from all over the world to study with you—do you employ some of Casals's teaching techniques?

B.G.: My style of teaching is, I think, quite different. I try to teach the craft first. I believe there is a science to playing the instrument which has nothing to do with the musical gift. My first emphasis with a student is to help him overcome the difficulties of the instrument. It's a study, almost a science—and only when I feel he has mastered the instrument sufficiently will I make "musical" suggestions.

Int.: Yet those who come to study with you cannot be described as beginners. They probably believe they are competent in what you call the "craft."

B.G.: There is no one who doesn't have problems on the instrument. If we are honest we'll admit to problems whether we are performing concert artists or students at the conservatory level.

Int.: So your first responsibility as teacher is to diagnose the weak spots in technique. Could you give an example of that, and how you would propose a remedy?

B.G.: The techniques of playing the cello have changed tremendously since the days of Feuermann and Casals. There was a time, for instance, when the stretches presented great difficulties on the instrument. The fourth finger was used to a great extent in the upper reaches of the instrument—the hand was forced into an abnormal position of stretching because of the distances between notes. We have learned in recent years a new technique of moving the hand on the fingerboard without the great effort of stretching the fingers. You find that one of the major problems with young people is precisely this strain of the left hand and in the bow arm. I try to eliminate that, to make the performance as easy and as natural as possible. The concentration should be on musical ideas rather than on the instrument as such. When I perform today, I find that I am not even aware of the cello in front of me. My concentration is entirely on something else; I sing the phrase before it is produced. I hear it in my mind and I get ideas for how to perform that phrase before it comes out of the instrument. And so the challenge is to be able to produce it without having to concentrate on how it's been produced. It has to come out naturally. It must flow out of the instrument.

Int.: So the space between intention and performance becomes in effect nonexistent?

B.G.: Yes. I would compare it in a very simple way to learning how to drive a car with manual transmission, or learning how to brake. You see a car in front of you, and you must make a short stop. You don't think, Well, I'd better put my foot down on the brake now. All the movements become natural, though at some point they had to be learned. Shifting and braking—they're part of the body, and in this case the bodily extension, a car.

Int.: But if somebody has the habit of putting his foot on the accelerator when he believes he's going to brake . . .

B.G.: That's where I come in. That's when you start to teach him how—forgive the pun—to break the habit. And you must say things in many different ways in order to get an idea across clearly. This confusion can sometimes last for weeks, until you have found the right manner of expressing the change. But once you have found it—and once he has recognized the progress—the technique is likely to stick. And only then, only much later do you start to diagnose sensitivity: how to produce colors with the bow, how to make a phrase more poignant by changing the "inspiration." I believe that this is much more difficult to do.

Int.: To return to those lessons you had with Casals, is this the "second hour"—the discussion of musical ideas?

B.G.: Yes. There are so many ways of producing a reaction on the instrument and in the listener. The easiest way is just to read the music; the most difficult is to realize that there are hundreds of choices available in a phrase. And you have to choose the one which is not only suitable for your own character, your own way of expression, but the one that will communicate—will convey your interpretation to the audience.

Int.: In the case of the cello literature, however, there are very few instructions to the musician. Bach comes unadorned. Boccherini—who must have been a great technician to be able to perform his pieces—doesn't tell you how to replicate his own techniques. So part of the task must be, I would imagine, to construe yourself as the original performer. How much leeway does this allow for interpretation, and how various can the performances be?

B.G.: With the Bach Suites, the latitude is enormous. There are at least thirty editions of the Bach Suites, and the author of each is certain he has found the answer. I can only refer back to Casals, who brought the Bach Suites into prominence in concert. He made a set of the six Bach Suites for RCA many years ago, but never listened to them afterwards. He said he couldn't stand hearing them because he would never play them the same way one hour after completion. Now there is a great latitude in the performance of Bach—more so, even, than with Boccherini. Boccherini has written dynamic marks where he wants a *forte*, it's marked on the page so that one must stay with the score. But even remaining within the score provides movement in music. And this movement, if it does not distort the rhythm, is essential to interpretation. You can stay with the *forte*, you can stay with the *piano*, the crescendo, the diminuendo—that's just reading the score. But interpretation is something much more intricate, much more refined. You can open the image of a sonata of Beethoven's in a thousand different ways, with emphasis on different notes within the phrase, with movement, with color in sound . . .

Int.: Would you feel, however, that there is a rigidity within that randomness? Is it permissible, for instance, to play a note *piano* that has been marked *forte?*

B.G.: No, that's not possible. But the gradation of the *forte* is up to the individual. If you have a *forte* and three bars later, you have a *fortissimo* and a crescendo, then your *forte* must be in proportion to the *fortissimo* which is about to arrive. Also, as I said before, there is movement within the phrase. You must have what I call the domino feeling. You line up dominoes, and then you push the first one and there's a forward motion which brings them all down. The danger with students especially is that you make a suggestion of this kind, and they immediately change the tempo and distort. When you listen to a great artist like Horowitz, part of the tremendous excitement which he engenders comes through the motion of the music. And the reverse is also true. In a *tranquillo*, a quiet passage, the feeling of drawing back without distorting the tempo—this can also influence a receptive audience. You can hear them breathe a sigh and feel tranquillity more than if you kept the steady metronomic tempo.

If I were to consider a career on the instrument today, and I listened to the enormous number of young gifted cellists—gifted at least in the technical sense—I'd hesitate. The techniques have improved so much, and there are so many accomplished young cellists by now. When I was a student there might have been twenty young cellists at the Curtis and the Juilliard; today there are hundreds. The teaching has been superior. We have garnered in this country the finest of gifted cello performers and professors. We have people like [Janos] Starker and Leonard Rose; we have people on the West Coast like Gabor Rejto; we have Zara Nelsova and Bonnie Hampton; we've had Piatigorsky teaching a superior class of students. What I want to stress, though, is that—however much techniques may have changed—talent has not progressed. Talent remains something which one cannot instruct or invent. And while there are many, many great instrumentalists, one has to search for the true artist—that great talent we encounter so rarely. They are still quite as rare as they were fifty or one hundred or two hundred years ago.

Int.: Is it necessary for the teacher of an instrument to be a virtuoso? The teaching of voice, for instance, does not always demand that those who coach singers are or have been better singers than their students. Their demonstration of technique is geared to no audience but the student.

B.G.: The student has to want, and desperately, to be better than his master. Gregor Piatigorsky told me a story about a very gifted student whom he found it hard to teach. Every time he demonstrated how he wanted a phrase played, the student would play worse. And as the lessons went on, the student's playing deteriorated till Gregor decided to try something new. He would demonstrate a phrase but play it badly. And each time he played badly the student played it better. This went on until finally the student gained the confidence that he could outplay his master, and finally Piatigorsky had the right approach. It takes that kind of insight, that sense of each student as an individual.

Int.: Are the students of famous teachers possessed of a recognizable sound? Can you tell on first hearing that such and such a violinist is a student of Ivan Galamian?

B.G.: Not in his case. All his students have enormous facility on the instrument, yet each retains personality. There is no mold set for the player. Today many young people will form a loyalty to a particular teacher, and to the exclusion of others. Very often the funneling of talent into a source will also make the reputation of a teacher, and then you have the best talents arriving from all over the world. My own approach to teaching has been different. I was a professor at Juilliard for many years, and I've taught and still teach at first-rate schools. But my experience has been with young people who were not, for the most part, world-shaking talents. And I have always felt that these people need fine teaching as much if not more than the great talents. Therefore I have varied the quality of my class; I have accepted students who I've felt were desperately in need of fine teaching. That sounds egotistical, but I feel I can help with problems on the instrument; the progress is less manifest if they come to you full-formed.

Universities have opened new avenues for careers. There are many more universities now that have a quartet or trio in residence, and many of the smaller cities in the U.S.A. have formed professional orchestras or small opera companies. As the number of aspiring professionals are turned out at the major conservatories and universities, the opportunities also are broadened. So I believe a young person who is driven to a career in music will eventually find a place for himself. I have taught perhaps two or three hundred cellists, and I can't think of more than two or three who have not found a place for themselves in the professional world.

Int.: You sound like a man still in love with his work. Is that true?

B.G.: I would not have done anything else. Performance changes; generations change their strategy. We can listen to an old recording of one of the famous quartets and be astonished at the methods they used—the way they used glissandi, for instance, hurts our ears today. And since I am now of the older generation I must hear what the young people are doing in order to make my playing stay as modern and contemporary as possible. There may still be a variance in my ideas of interpretation, but I try as much as possible to keep up with my young gifted students. They are a source of energy and enthusiasm which I would not miss for anything. Once you have a love of music, you're stuck with it the rest of your life. It becomes as essential as food.

Chapter Three

"If I'd known then what I know now," Tom Johnson says. "If I'd had any idea . . ." He laughs, his head thrown back. "I just didn't know what it meant." He gestures to the folders full of correspondence, the message slips and ticket orders and charge forms that clutter his table. "I didn't know the first thing about it, I just picked up the phone and called Columbia Artists and asked about a concert in this town."

When the Trio walk out onstage, it is as if they materialize from the thin air of the wings. They wear white tie and vest, black patent leather shoes, and tails. They appear well fed and washed; what hair they have has been barbered. Two of the men carry instruments, and all three carry music. At a distance, a page turner follows. The performers acknowledge applause. They sit, adjust their chairs slightly, and arrange their music on the stands. The lights have dimmed or blinked to signal to the audience that the concert will begin—the audience sitting in prearranged seats. The hall is, more often than not, sold out; it has been rented long in advance, and ushers distribute literature that indicates the evening's program. There are, perhaps, program notes. This magical-seeming conjunction—performers, place, time, audience—is not of course spontaneous. It has been planned. These pages will describe, in detail, the presentation of one such concert—what thickens the air in the wings.

Some concerts prove more problematic than others to present. There may be airline strikes, snowstorms, sickness, an unsatisfactory piano or hall. No two afternoons or evenings are alike. Yet by and large the fabric of performance feels seamless; the Trio and their audience focus their attention on music, and music alone. In this regard it makes no difference if the place is Buenos Aires or Birmingham, Kyoto or Cardiff or Seattle or Rome. The logistics vary but the logic is the same. However noisy the previous hour, there must be silence when the program starts. The anticipatory bustle will be different in each instance, but the desired consequence is constant: a poised peace.

On October 25, 1982, the Beaux Arts Trio performed in Sanders Theater, Cambridge, Massachusetts. The time was 8:00 P.M.. The "local presentor"—a contractual term—was the Winthrop House Music Society of Harvard University, and this concert was the first in a series of four. The subsequent concerts would take place in December 1982, and in February and April 1983. The trio series highlighted Brahms, since the composer had been born in 1833, and this season represented the hundred and fiftieth anniversary of his birth. The program consisted of the Mozart Trio in C Major, K. 548; the Schumann Trio No. 2 in F Major, Op. 80; and, after intermission, the Brahms Trio in B Major, Op. 8. The Trio arrived in Boston the late morning of the twenty-fifth; they would leave the following day.

Tom Johnson has anticipated this one day for months. He is an old hand at it now; this is the fourteenth Beaux Arts concert he has presented in Cambridge. At thirty-two, he is an unlikely seeming "old hand," and his professional expertise is self-taught; his is a cottage industry. Since Winthrop House itself is under reconstruction, Johnson's apartment on Garden Street in Cambridge doubles as an office. The dining alcove has a pair of telephones (one with his private number, one with an answering service), and electric typewriter, and an adding machine; the tabletop is strewn with charge-card forms and brochures. Open cartons line the floor. There are mailing lists, subscription lists, stamp rolls, records of who gets which seat. His furniture is spare: a low bed, a stereo set and cabinet of records, two rubber plants. A set of weights lies in the corner, and an upturned out-of-commission five-speed Raleigh bicycle. "That's for errands in Cambridge," he says. "Your everyday knockabout bike. This one"—he points to a sleek blue Fuji—"that's for when I'm serious."

Born in Dayton, Ohio, Tom Johnson entered Harvard College with the class of 1972. His great love is the piano, and he found himself spending longer and longer periods in the practice room; he transferred to the New England Conservatory of Music and was graduated in 1974. He then returned to Harvard as "artist-in-residence" at Winthrop House—one of the thirteen colleges within the college where upperclassmen reside. He also began commuting to Bloomington, Indiana, in order to study piano with Menahem Pressler; and he traveled to New York and elsewhere in order to hear the Trio. He is an unabashed fan.

The Trio had not performed in Boston, however, for years. Records indicate one performance (sponsored by the Harvard summer school in Sanders) on August 13, 1962, and one under the auspices of the Boston University Celebrity Series on January 31, 1971. This latter appearance had been greeted with a less than rapturous review; the presentor had not invited them next season, and Boston dropped out of the itinerary.

Tom Johnson determined to change that. He called Columbia Artists Management, Inc., in April 1978. Then began the lengthy process of persuasion; he had to convince a skeptical series of respondents that he was in earnest. It is harder to acquire the Trio for a first engagement than to invite them back; the major proportion of their appearances (by now as much as 90 percent) are "repeats." And Johnson was a maverick as well as tyro in the field; he knew Pressler but did not enlist his help. Only when the contracts were in hand did he inform the Trio that his efforts had born fruit.

The file is thick. After several conversations with Hattie Clark, who oversees all such negotiations in the CAMI Building, Johnson was granted permission, on April 28, to present a concert on November 6. The name of Harvard helped. Though the university offered no official assistance, the Winthrop House Music Society lent credibility to Johnson's requests. One Harvard official did offer a personal financial guarantee. Discussion was protracted—but by October 21, Johnson's letters begin "Dear Hattie," and he is proposing a Beethoven cycle for a concert series in 1979. The Trio's reputation had enlarged since they were last in Boston, and their prolonged absence helped generate enthusiasm: the concert sold out. This has been true ever since.

Sanders Theater in Memorial Hall is the largest assembly space in Cambridge. With 131 stage seats included, there are more than 1300 tickets to be sold. (The other two plausible concert spaces—Symphony Hall and Jordan Hall—were ruled out early on. The first is too cavernous for chamber music; the second, with approximately a thousand seats, less large than Johnson could fill. Their sites in downtown Boston remove them from the Harvard context, and the Winthrop House Music Society wanted the concert close to home.) Sanders Theater has history and atmosphere to commend it as well as first-rate acoustics. Henry

James described the structure as "consecrated to the sons of the university who fell in the long Civil War . . ." In *The Bostonians* (1886), he brings a character to

> . . . one place where perhaps it would be indelicate to take a Mississippian . . . the great place that towers above the others—that big building with the beautiful pinnacles, which you see from every point. . . . He thought there was rather too much brick about it, but it was buttressed, cloistered, turreted, dedicated, superscribed, as he had never seen anything; though it didn't look old, it looked significant; it covered a large area, and it sprang majestic into the winter air. It was detached from the rest of the collegiate group, and stood in a grassy triangle of its own . . .

That "grassy triangle" has given way to pavement now, and walkways over traffic. Yet the high theater paneled in wood leaves an "effect . . . singularly noble and solemn, and it is impossible to feel it without a lifting of the heart." Memorial Hall and Sanders Theater have, however, neither box office nor staff. The Winthrop House Music Society found itself therefore operating a promotional agency and ticket bureau. Tom Johnson says, with characteristic self-deprecation, that a fool could fill Sanders Theater when the Trio are in town. This may be so, but the "fool" must supervise a clutch of daily details, from seating manifest to mailing lists.

On Saturday before the concert, his phone rings continually. "No, I'm sorry," he repeats. "The concert is sold out." This was the case for the subscription list since June, and, since the previous Tuesday, for stage seats. If a caller is persistent or expresses disbelief, Johnson might encourage him to go to the theater the night of the concert; there may be last-minute returns, he says, someone who bought three tickets and is only using two. . . .

Winthrop House has been undergoing an extensive renovation; work crews have been at it all summer. The target date for completion was the start of Fall Semester, and part of the bargain has been kept. Were the three hundred students to have been boarded elsewhere, at university expense, the cost of delay might well have proved prohibitive—so the student rooms are ready for their September return. The heating and electrical systems have been totally reworked; the halls have been painted, floors sanded, plaster fixed.

Not so, however, with the Master's Residence. The Harvard house system includes residential space for tutors and a separate lodging for the "Master"—in this case, sociologist Jim Davis—and his family; the model is that of an extended family. Jim and Martha Davis are in effect the Trio's hosts, but they live in a construction site. Now the promised date of completion is December 1; the Davises hope to be able to celebrate Christmas in a refurbished home. Workmen swarm through the kitchen and halls where, that night, a reception will take place; the paint pots and grouting and ladders get shoved back out of sight. One recent casualty of renovation is the office of the Winthrop House Music Society; it holds drop cloths and lumber and tools.

Tom Johnson has moved out. He has taken the music society with him, temporarily; there is less clutter at home. Shorts and polo shirts hang drying in his shower stall; photographs of his family in Dayton and his married sister in Peterboro, New Hampshire, adorn the kitchen cabinets. He eats a baloney sandwich; his is a bachelor's life. One framed poster of the Trio hangs above the telephone. Whimsically—for it was a French performance—the Beaux Arts Trio have been Englished to "The Fine Arts Trio." He is also sponsoring a concert by the Orlando

String Quartet, with Pressler joining them for the Brahms Piano Quintet in F Minor. This ensemble, he assures callers, comes from Amsterdam, not Florida; they are on their North American debut tour. The concert will take place on election night, November 2. These tickets are difficult to sell, and much of Johnson's weekend is spent arranging radio ads for the subsequent week, doing a final mailing; it is clear autumn weather, and he takes two bike trips with posters under his arm.

The principal expenditures for a concert are threefold: rental of facilities, promotional and advertising expenses, and the artists' fees. The first and second are, in the case of the Trio, nominal; Harvard charges little rent for a weeknight series, and he barely needs to advertise. Every ticket has been sold. "The Beaux Arts," he asserts. "It's like slicing a sharp knife through butter. I could take the weekend off."

Robert J. Lurtsema's *Morning Pro Musica* originates in Boston. Perhaps the premier classical "disc jockey" in the nation, Lurtsema plays music five hours a morning, seven days a week, and discusses the selections mellifluously. His planning too is done long in advance, and he has scheduled a Haydn retrospective; 1982 is the three hundred and fiftieth anniversary of the composer's birth. From September through December, proceeding chronologically, he plays the Haydn Piano Trios before the nine o'clock news. For other such series—Mozart, Beethoven, Telemann—he samples various performances and representative groups. This is true of other aspects of the Haydn literature. But the Trio have completed, for Philips Records, a comprehensive set of the forty-three Haydn Piano Trios; Lurtsema departs from his usual practice and plays these exclusively. So every day since September his audience has heard the Trio perform. "Every time he plays the Haydn," Johnson says, "I get another call."

The concert manifest is a blue vinyl folder with the plan of Sanders Theater, and marked-in seating arrangements. The hall has been color coordinated (yellow, blue, and green according to ticket costs), and Johnson fills it in section by section. On the master manifest he inserts the dates of sale. The manifest contains the names of every ticket purchaser and when the tickets were mailed. He notes in addition how payment was made—by cash, credit card, or check. "Every once in a while," Johnson says, "there's a misplaced order. I have a file called 'Problems.' Someone claims they sent more than they sent, or forgot to add correctly. Or the number on their card's wrong, or maybe it expired. It's not often, two or three a concert maybe, nothing to plan for; concertgoers are honest."

Various, too; those who attend the performance have a cacophony of names. One section of seats reads, seriatim, like a demographer's report: Wheeler, Cardon, Simoncelli, Dingee, Hirsch, Distler, Lohrenz, Spiesberger, Fawcett, Garber, Lightbody, Mattes, Khajchadourian, Fabris, and Burns. Harvard names abound, from President Bok on down. There is a page of the booklet for "Guests": those who receive complimentary seats. Each member of the Trio gets two, as do the local papers and the classical music stations. This concert will go unreviewed. The papers are chock-full with music assignments, Johnson explains, and the Trio will play three more engagements; it's a Monday night. Review space is booked solid, he has been told, and last weekend's concerts will run through Wednesday, maybe Thursday of the week. So the first notice would be Friday, and by that time it's next weekend, it isn't worth it to push. . . .

Things are not that simple. As with many other artists, insults rankle where praise is dismissed. The proportion of compliment to dispraise for the Beaux Arts Trio is disproportionate: for fifty raves they receive one pan. But the reviewer for the *Boston Globe* savaged a concert they gave two summers earlier at Tanglewood; he assaulted their performance of the Beethoven Triple Concerto from the first note to the last. Without going so far as to exclude the offending party from the hall, Johnson does not urge him to attend (as, for instance, he will do for the Orlando String Quartet). It is hard to resist taking potshots at a group at their profession's peak; the competition is fierce. Reviews of the Trio can do, at present, nothing to swell their reputation or audience; they are icing on the cake. But negative reaction could, over time and cumulatively, hurt.

On Monday the Trio arrive. They have played in Manhattan on Saturday night; in Ossining, New York, on Sunday. Greenhouse and his wife, Aurora, have used the occasion of proximity to their elder daughter to spend the night in Hartford, Connecticut; on Monday morning they come to Cambridge by car. Cohen and Pressler returned to Manhattan after the Sunday concert and have taken the shuttle to Boston, arriving on the noon flight. Tom Johnson collects them at Logan. Small-scale disruptions occur. The flight from New York is delayed—trouble with a cargo door—and the next night's performance has been canceled. Their schedule had called for arrival on Tuesday in New Haven, and a concert sponsored by the New Haven Symphony Orchestra. Those musicians, however, are out on strike—and the Trio do not wish to cross the picket line. Management of the New Haven Symphony concurs, and the engagement has been postponed; at some later date they will perform a substitute concert. They make jokes about the "friendly persuasion" of the musicians' union, which requested that they cancel; broken cellos, snapped bows, and concertgoers with tommy guns figure in the wit.

The three musicians stay in Winthrop House, in a series of guest suites. Martha Davis apologizes for the work crew and the wreckage everywhere; they assure her all's well. When Greenhouse unpacks his suitcase, however, he discovers he's left his dress suit behind—in his daughter's closet in Hartford. Such forgetfulness is rare; they live in constant fear of leaving music stands or music or cameras behind them in hotels. He has white tie and vest and shirt and shoes, but neither the tails nor the pants. They are hanging in Connecticut and cannot be retrieved. Greenhouse is sheepish but unalarmed. "If this were Iowa," he says, "or Florida, Nebraska—anywhere but Cambridge—I'd have trouble finding tails. But here"—he spreads his hands. Martha Davis accepts the challenge, promising dress clothes his size.

After lunch (the Greenhouses with their grandchildren at One Potato, Two Potato in Harvard Square; Pressler and Cohen with Johnson in a Chinese restaurant), the dress suit is produced. It more or less fits across the shoulders, but the pants are far too tight. Greenhouse wonders if he could perform in his gray flannel pants, passing muster with just the black top. Martha Davis demurs. Having secured his measurements, she telephones the formal-wear outlets in Cambridge; one suit is pressed and waiting. The others in the Trio are relieved; they play in suits on afternoons, but dress clothes only at night. "Should we get him a black suit?" my wife, Elena, asks. "Or a maroon, or mauve, or midnight blue?" Pressler is alarmed. "We *always* play in black."

Cambridge Formal Wear contains long racks of suits—tuxedos, dinner jackets, morning coats, tails. They extend the length of the second floor in a rundown walk-up building across from Porter Square Shopping Center. The card reads: "Merged—Sam & Bill's (Est. 1917)." "What about accessories?" the salesman asks. "You sure you don't need none?" He waves at the sunburst of color: ranked rows. A set of black tails, swathed in plastic, hangs before the mirror. Back at Winthrop House, it fits. There is some slack at the waist, and Greenhouse puts his thumb there proudly. Cloth at the waistline protrudes. "Look at that," he says. "I could get another person in." "You'd better not," says Pressler. "It looks a lot more classy than what you have from Hong Kong."

They have played before this audience and performed these pieces often. They are nothing if not professional, and this is one day's work. Yet through the day there is a gathering tension, an inward focus on the concert soon to come. That afternoon Pressler and Cohen practice—separately—in Winthrop House; Greenhouse, weary after driving, takes a nap. Mrs. Pressler never travels with the Trio, and the other two wives do so only rarely; the men are not free-ranging tourists. Tom Johnson collects them at six. Students have attended to last-minute details: making sure the hall is open, making sure its temperature is adequate, making sure the stage seats are in place and a program waits on every seat. He is proud of this last touch. "You can only do it if the concert's sold out," Johnson explains. "But it saves time for the ushers, and it makes the audience feel welcome when they sit."

Since the Trio are familiar with Sanders Theater, and Pressler trusts the piano there, they need allot no time to deal with unanticipated trouble. CAMI has provided stage directions in advance—though these are by now second nature to Johnson. The sheet is a checklist: "*Page turner:* Required; *Lighting:* Even overhead lighting desired, no footlights, no direct spots, no colored gels (plain white); *Piano:* Steinway concert grand (9 foot) and adjustable piano bench. The lid will be on half stick for Trios; *Music Stands:* The Artists carry their own; *Chairs:* Two straight-backed chairs required for the violinist and the cellist; requests for backstage 'drinking water or soft drinks or coffee' and rehearsal time 'starting about one hour before the public is admitted.' The piano should have been tuned before they rehearse and have a 'touch-up' after the rehearsal is over (if possible)." This rehearsal is brief. By seven the first concertgoers arrive, and the Trio withdraw backstage. The piano tuner does indeed return; he is finished by seven-fifteen.

"Backstage" at Sanders Theater is the large, ill-heated Memorial Hall. Henry James called it "a vast refectory, covered with a timbered roof, hung about with portraits and lighted by stained windows . . ."; undergraduates at Harvard have registered for courses and taken exams there for years. The light is dim. There is no private bathroom for the artists. Johnson has provided crackers, ginger ale, hot coffee, and Perrier; the Trio never eat before performing. A glass of wine, says Greenhouse, can cost you an hour of coordination; a sandwich can ruin a piece.

Fourteen Winthrop House students are on hand to help. They have signed up as ushers in exchange for a free ticket and an invitation to the reception later on. Johnson has provided three sheets of single-space instructions for his ushers and ticket takers. It is a curious document—hortatory, personal, and assuming a literate crew. In it he describes routine procedure and anticipates emergency; here are some sample paragraphs:

> You need not take everyone to their seats. Only escort some directly to their seats if they have some physical difficulty or if they seem unusually confused.
>
> LATECOMERS: FLOOR ushers 23 & 24, PARQUET ushers A & G, and BALCONY ushers A & G have the honor of glaring at late people through the glass doors (and shake your head in the "No" direction) if they seem to be on the verge of entering before the music stops (they have been instructed by the ticket takers NOT to enter until it stops, but sometimes temptation becomes too great!). As soon as the music stops at the end of a movement, all of a sudden become these folks' best friends, smile, and nod "yes." (Do as much of this nodding business from your seat as possible—even though it may feel a little awkward. Your getting up and walking around on the creaky floors in Sanders will make as much noise as someone coming in . . .)
>
> MEN'S ROOM—Parquet Balcony G end of hall, across the lobby, next to the phone booth.
> WOMEN'S ROOM—Parquet Balcony A end of hall, under the parquet stairs on the FLOOR level.
> PHONE—by the entrance to the MEN'S ROOM.
> DRINKING FOUNTAINS—in the rest rooms.
>
> DR. LUCIEN LEAPE (Marty's husband) sits in front of PARQUET D (seats 88–91). In case of MEDICAL EMERGENCY, try if possible to help the person out of the concert hall as quietly as possible. If not possible to move the person, get a doctor as calmly and quietly as possible.
>
> SORRY: ticket colors do not correspond to seat *location* in any manner easily explainable. Colors correspond to ticket *price*. Look at the ticket! I just mention colors, because if you en-

counter one outside of tonight's pre-determined rainbow, someone's at the wrong concert.

At six it starts to rain. The rain is unremitting. "We always play Cambridge in rain," Cohen says. Tom Johnson reminds him that once it snowed instead, and the Trio played in boots. Cohen says the damp might help the sound, though the acoustics in Sanders are fine. He talks about the old days, recording sessions in New York where the studio was so dry, the air so cracklingly unkind to instruments that they turned on every shower on the floor. "When the steam got thick enough," he says, "when you couldn't see the page in front of you, we'd turn off the showers and play."

Greenhouse, lighting a cigar, explains the program choice. It has been determined months before. (Johnson proposed the dates for the 1982–83 season in a letter to Hattie Clark on September 15, 1981—and this letter was a confirmation of previous discussions.) "It's like a Chinese restaurant," says Greenhouse. "We offer one from Column A, one from Column B, and one from Column C; then the presentor buys the meal. Sometimes he knows what he wants beforehand, sometimes we might make suggestions. We start with something light, Hummel or Haydn or Mozart. And the main course this series is Brahms. For the second work we offer something spicy—Shostakovitch, maybe, Ives, Ravel. But Schumann was a major influence on Brahms. 'Gentleman, an eagle is among us!' Didn't he say that? Something like it anyway, when he first heard Brahms. 'My love,' he wrote Clara, 'you must hear this. Such music as you have never before listened to!'"

In the arching vestibule, the crowd is thick. Some have come to sell an extra ticket; some, in the hope of last-minute cancellations, come to buy. The subscription list, Johnson explains, is 95 percent from the greater Boston area. This is a weekday crowd, he says, they're coming from work. A few arrive from out of state—from Rhode Island, maybe, or Maine. The regulars know they have to buy their series tickets in advance—but how can you tell, in April, if you're certain to be free one Monday in October? So there are always a few who change plans, a few who take advantage of the change. But by and large, he says, a thousand people in the room have seen each other here before; they won't know each other to talk to, of course, in spite of what you may have heard, not everyone knows everyone in Cambridge. . . .

The preperformance buzz and hum feels nonetheless familial. People nod and wave and shake hands as they enter, and there is shuffling in the aisles where friends greet friends. A dean here, a patron there, a Nobel laureate or Boston media personality—Johnson, at the gate, appears to know them all. They talk about the weather, the stock market, the elections; several say, "*Aimez-vous Brahms?*"

At eight o'clock they clog the aisles; there are two ticket entrances, with two levels of entry at each. Many of the ushers show less familiarity with row locations than do the regular subscribers. Students point professors to their seats. The doors at each end of the wide central hall stand ajar; rain gleams in the puddles beyond. The hall itself feels cold. It has no cloakroom facilities, and several elder patrons complain about umbrellas and wet coats. Predictably, however, such conversation slackens and people find their seats.

At seven minutes after eight, Sanders Theater is replete; the stage seats, too, have been filled. Johnson collects the Trio, walks them to the stage door, and offers his ritual good-luck gesture: thumbs up. (He would not say, "Break a leg!" because it brings back memories; Greenhouse had in fact broken a leg the previous season. He fell on an ice-covered porch in Wellfleet, one week before a European tour. It was too late to cancel or find a replacement, and he played twenty-two concerts in a cast. Johnson traveled with the Beaux Arts, helping with the wheelchair and the crutches and the instrument.) He dims the lights and takes his own seat—Parquet C–106. It is, he says, the first chance he has had to scan the house; he relishes that moment, unamazed.

The Trio appear. They come out buoyantly, smiling—first Pressler, then Greenhouse, then Cohen. They take a brief bow to acknowledge applause, and they sit. They deposit music on the thin metallic stands; they have left the stands but not the music onstage after rehearsal. Since they have just completed tuning, Pressler sounds no note. The page turner waits by the piano. She has evidently chosen a folding chair and set it by a piano bench. The stage manager earlier had positioned three straight-backed brocade chairs; this leaves one untenanted seat. They begin.

The Mozart C Major Trio, K. 548, was written in the summer of 1788. Sandwiched between the masterful E-flat and G Minor symphonies, it seems slight not merely by comparison. Mozart's piano trios are composed for amateur performance—although in the eighteenth century the distance between amateur and professional appears to have been small. He deploys the virtuoso-concertante style, and it is a fine warm-up piece; the third movement, the "French" Rondo, is a crowd pleaser and was likely intended as such. It conveys no disrespect to Mozart's astonishing genius to call this piano trio casual; it demands comparatively little of the musicians and audience. Seventeen minutes long, it is—to shift the cuisine in Greenhouse's metaphor of a Chinese meal—an "hors d'oeuvre." The Trio play well, but with a sense throughout of power-in-reserve. The listeners feel that way also, and their response is dutiful; they have come here for Schumann and Brahms.

In 1847, Robert Schumann composed his D Minor and F Major piano trios. They are among his major contributions to chamber music literature, and the Trio No. 2—as Schumann wrote Carl Reinecke, with particular reference to the second and third movements—is one of which he was proud. Both ambitious and achieved, it makes substantial demands of the performers; the primacy, in Schumann's early work, of the pianoforte here gives way to a strict and consistent balance. Hanspeter Krellman (in program notes for the Beaux Arts recording of Schumann) puts it as follows: "These two trios mark a new stand in chamber music, and not merely in that of Schumann. Apart from the individuality of the musical invention and the thematic material, apart from the mastery of the form and the detailed working-out of the themes, including much contrapuntal intertwining—in fact, an altogether polyphonic treatment—we can recognise a new kind of expressiveness, attained by the use of suspensions, exactly calculated interval relationships, and taut rhythms. None of this had been found before, in either Beethoven or Schubert. In both trios Schumann emerges primarily as an intellectual composer."

The classical attributes of Schumann argued above, and brought forth by the composer's recent extensive study of Bach, run nonetheless counter to the more common notion of Schumann as a tormented, intermittently rational, and principally intuitive artist. The F Major Trio presents a kind of counterpoise; it is a blend of modes and moods not easily attained.

That the Beaux Arts meets the challenge seems the audience consensus; here the applause is prolonged. What constitutes definitive interpretation is of course a matter of opinion, and opinions vary. But the talk at intermission is excited, elated. One gentleman recites Schumann's instructions for the movements: *Zehr lebhaft; Mit innigem Ausdruck; in Mässiger Bewegung; Nicht zu rasch.* They have been followed to the letter, he exclaims; his German accent is good. A few folk remain in their seats. A few pursue the Trio backstage—Robert J. Lurtsema among them—but most crowd to the lobby: smoking, chatting, catching up. The piano tuner inquires of Pressler if everything's all right; Pressler thanks him, yes.

Brahms's Trio in B major, Op. 8, comes next. Originally written in 1853 and 1854, it was extensively reworked in 1889; jokingly, having indulged his penchant for revision, he called it Op. 108. The Trio play, and have recorded, the second version of the piece; Clara Schumann—Robert's widow and Brahms's inspiration if not inamorata—would have approved. She wrote of the original composition (the first of Brahms's published chamber works) that "I could only wish for another first movement as the present one does not satisfy me, although I admit that its opening is fine." Before publication of the new version, however, she wrote, "The Trio seems to me to be a complete success."

From the extended melody with which the piece begins to the coda with which it rounds off, Op. 8 is vintage Brahms. And though there have been twenty intervening minutes since the last note of the Schumann, this sounds like a continuum: the line of ascent feels unbroken. The lyric power of the strings and the almost martial emphasis in the piano make this a showpiece for the Beaux Arts, a soaring romantic assertion. There seems no distance from intention to execution; the Trio have the audience entirely with them by now.

The encore is the Scherzo from Beethoven's Op. 1, No. 1. The concert is a manifest success. The line where the performers receive praise is long. The rain has slackened; their spirits are high. "Not too much romantic music?" Cohen asks, and everyone assures him that the pairing of Schumann and Brahms was ideal. The musicians put away their instruments; they empty the Perrier. There are programs to sign, family and friends to greet; old students report on progress. Greenhouse lights up a cigar. "Schumann," muses Pressler. "Even in his madness he was noble; most people when they're schizophrenic, if they're institutionalized, there's a certain"—he hunts the word—"vulgarity. But Schumann even mad was complicated, noble. The more noble of the two, I think, though Brahms was of course more achieved."

They repair to Winthrop House. The Master's Residence—or the visible sections thereof—has been transformed. Where, earlier, a mason warned that nobody could walk, the floor seems rock-firm now; where a banister came loose in the hand, it has been tacked upright. Students throng the living room; there are dry white wine and cheese. Cohen changes back to street clothes; the other two retain their dress pants and vests, but wear sports jackets instead of tails. It is eleven o'clock. They accept large chunks of cheese, drinks, plaudits; the students manage to appear both awestruck and aloof. Martha Davis has dinner waiting in the kitchen, but the Trio linger in the living room. A framed autographed poster sent back from the last

European tour—some unpronounceable town outside of Amsterdam—is propped up in the hall. Several students attempt to pronounce it. Jim Davis expatiates on the renovation process. "Mostly it's a question of heating and wiring," he says. "Some radiators were locked open; you'd have to keep the windows open or you'd die of steam. In others there just wasn't heat. Look at all that plaster work"—he points to the molding, its complicated contours—"there's miles of that in here."

Just before midnight, Martha Davis collects the Trio, insisting they must eat. Tom Johnson too has a place—at the head of the table, the Trio decide. Aurora Greenhouse joins the party; there are five chairs. They eat heartily: chicken in a white cream sauce, rice, green salad, celery remoulade, bread. There are Rheinwein and Champagne. Cohen tells the joke about the doctor's dog, the engineer's dog, the lawyer's dog, and how the three emulate their owners' skills. I tell my Lufthansa joke: a plane crash-lands at sea; the passengers, obedient, swim in unison. Elena tells the joke about two women on the park bench. One turns to the other and says, "So, tell me, Bessie, what do you think of Red China?" Bessie ponders. "On a yellow tablecloth it's fine." Everyone laughs hugely; tomorrow will be a free day. Pressler had intended to meet his daughter in New Haven; she attends Smith College and could have driven from Northampton. But now that New Haven has canceled, he must make alternative plans.

Tom Johnson is transported; he says, repeatedly, that this concert was the best. He has sponsored fourteen Trio appearances in Sanders Theater, and they take his compliment seriously. Greenhouse requests a cigar. The presentor has bought four Partagas; he produces them with a flourish. Cohen pockets his; the other two light up. Fritz Kreisler—

or so goes the story—was invited by a society matron to perform at a house party. He said his fee was four thousand dollars; she called it stiff but agreed. "Of course you understand," she added as an afterthought, "you'll eat with staff in the kitchen. Not with the invited guests." "In that case," Kreisler is reported to have said, "my fee for the performance is three thousand dollars."

At one-thirty, the Trio retire. Tom Johnson helps clean up. "I won't say the concert was wasted," he says, "not on this audience. But it ought to change your life. A concert like this one, like the Trio played tonight, it's *important*." He empties the wine. "Definitive. Definitive Schumann and Brahms. What I'd really like to do, sometime, is give all the tickets away. Give them to the bus drivers, every bus driver and cabbie in Boston. Can you imagine?"—he gestures, expansive—"there'd be no more honking, no more bad manners in town. Every single person would be improved who hears it. They'd wait for little old ladies, they'd make a *point* of waiting. I guarantee it," he says. "How can you live without being improved, elated by music like this? That crowd—they've just heard something absolute, a statement of complete artistic control. It washes over you."

Chapter Four

Isidore Cohen was born in Brooklyn, New York, on December 16, 1922. His early experience of music is described at some length in what follows; he studied under Ivan Galamian at the Juilliard School of Music. He has taught chamber music at Juilliard and the Curtis Institute, violin at the Mannes School of Music and the State University of New York at Stony Brook. He was a founding member of the Schneider String Quartet. His activity in the chamber music field has included guest appearances with the Budapest String Quartet, a second-violin position with the Juilliard String Quartet—and ongoing participation in Music at Marlboro. He replaced the original violinist of the Beaux Arts Trio, Daniel Guilet, in 1969 on Guilet's retirement.

This interview took place at the Cohens' newly acquired summer home in Marlboro, Vermont—the home, earlier, of the cellist Madeline Foley. Isidore and Judy Cohen have two children, Erica and Allen; they have been coming to Marlboro since the early 1960s. During my series of visits they were busy planting, painting—full of proprietary enthusiasm for their white house on the hill. Cohen is a natural raconteur. He started out displaying "my collection of succulents" and ended with a discourse on the horrors of vivisection. These transcriptions can but hope to evoke his broad range of accents, his articulate intensity, and responsive wit. Again my questions are signaled by the abbreviation "Int.," his answers by his initials "I.C."

Int.: Could you talk a little about your first exposure to music?

I.C.: I got a fiddle because my cousin started studying the

fiddle. We lived quite close to one another, in Brooklyn, and I used to spend time just listening to him practice. The bug got to me, and I loved what he was doing, I was very jealous—so I convinced my parents to get me a fiddle.

Int.: They had no previously expressed inclination to do that?

I.C.: No, not necessarily. I think my grandmother on my father's side was the most musical member of the family. When we went to the Second Avenue Theater, I'd sit next to her and always hear her humming; she would hum in the musical parts and sometimes too in the nonmusical parts. We were of Polish-Russian origin, and when I saw my family at weddings or a birthday, there was a great rhythmic impetus; they would start dancing—the Russian *kazatzky* or something similar—and they would burst into song. They enjoyed music, they loved it, but there was no inclination to formal study.

Int.: How, then, did your studies begin?

I.C.: I must have been somewhere between ten and eleven. That's a little bit late, you know, I should have started at three or four if I really wanted to accomplish something. I attended public schools and the High School of Music and Art, then went on to Brooklyn College. Mama wanted me to be a doctor; at Brooklyn College I was a science major, a premed. But I remember I went to the school orchestra rehearsals—and I was so jealous of those kids playing in the orchestra that I auditioned. By God, they made me concertmaster. But I was going to be a doctor; then I was drafted after two years of school, and World War II made me decide to be a musician. It was the first real break with my family aside from going to camp in the summer; I had always been very close to my parents. And something happened in the war, the misery of it. . . . At one point in France I was able to trade a pistol for a violin. I bought some music and started to practice; it gave me such pleasure, I decided, if I ever got out of this in one piece, I won't be a doctor, I'll study music.

Int.: How did the army feel about your trading that pistol?

I.C.: Well, it was a Spanish pistol. I traded it with a submarine man, a French submarine man; he had a short bow so he could practice in the submarine. Somewhere I have a picture of me out in a field in southern France, practicing, playing with this full-sized violin and a foot-long bow. And one day some people heard me playing in the field, and they said, you sound pretty good, we're trying to get into an army symphony orchestra; can we include your name? The whole thing was astonishing; I was asked to join the GI Symphony. And there I heard people who studied with this man, Galamian, from New York. I admired the playing of his students, and I thought, well, when I get back I'll take the GI Bill and study with the man. And again it worked out, it was a dream come true. I found out later that Mr. Galamian took me only because he felt it was his duty to have one veteran in his class. Mr. Galamian had the pick of the young talents, and I was much older—I must have been twenty-three, twenty-four. He liked to get them very young and shape them to his musical demands, his technical demands. Once, however, when he was pleased by something I had played, he told me he was happy about what had happened to me, but that when I first came to him he had accepted me as a patriotic obligation.

Int.: You must have worked hard those years, playing, in effect, "catch-up." I notice you called him "this man, Galamian," from a distance and "Mr. Galamian" when close. . . . How would you describe his teaching methods, and what were your habits as a student?

I.C.: He was my first serious teacher. I use the word "serious" in the sense that his demands were extreme. Before that I'd been studying, but I had no intention of becoming a professional musician. I loved it, and so I spent what time I had in practicing and doing chamber music, orchestra, whatever I could. But this was the first time I aspired to be a professional, and this was the man who could lead me. So six, seven, eight, nine hours just of practicing would not have been unusual. He demanded that kind of work from everybody anyway: four or five hours were the absolute minimum daily. Galamian was interested principally in the violin. Then came violin music, then music in general. And he was a man with a noble objective. When I used to bring in repertoire with which he was unhappy—or unfamiliar because it was either very modern or very very old—he'd say, all right, look, I will give you the means with which to do whatever *you* want to do. That's enough for me. Any teacher who can give you that is doing his job.

Int.: When did you first start earning a living in music, and how?

I.C.: At Juilliard I started doing some free-lancing, playing chamber music, and I managed to make money to supplement what I got from the GI Bill. Judy, my wife, always had a great deal of faith in me as a musician; it was through mutual friends who were musicians that we met. In retrospect I think Judy's support made it possible. Perhaps it was the cockiness of youth, but it never occurred to us that maybe this wouldn't work. When I graduated from Juilliard I joined the Schneider Quartet. There was a project to record—via the Haydn Society of Boston—all the works of Haydn: quartets, symphonies, trios, choral works, masses, the entire catalog. And so, in conjunction with Sascha Schneider, Karen Tuttle, and Madeline Foley, I performed all the quartets of Haydn. Depending on how you count, there are about eighty-seven of them. We never finished the project; we recorded about fifty, and then the Haydn Society went bankrupt. . . . But shortly after this, the second violin of the Juilliard Quartet left, and I was notified and asked to audition, then was invited to join. So I went right back to Juilliard and toured and played concerts with the Quartet for about ten years.

Int.: You must now be of an age roughly approximate to the age of Galamian when you were an ex-GI in his studio; do you find yourself patterning your teaching methods on his?

I.C.: His approach was a very fine one. Though he was very demanding in terms of time and technical demands, his approach to each student was different. It has to be; no two people are alike. You therefore can't say this is *my* way of thinking and everybody must accept it. It just won't work. His demands were extraordinary. There was something about Galamian's personality that gave you the impression, after a one-hour lesson, that you had been there for three—that three hours' work had been accomplished. I would like to be able to do that—both in working with ensembles and as a violin teacher—but I don't think I've achieved it, and I don't know what the secret is. . . .

My own orientation, my first love, is chamber music rather than solo repertoire. I am concerned with the musical ideas and emotional aspects of a particular passage rather than saying, hold the bow this way or tilt your left elbow and you will get the passage. Galamian came from a period when extreme demands on students' time—practicing up to ten hours a day—was considered standard. Nowadays we think there are other ways, other methods. It perhaps doesn't require this one way of working. The rounded life, the life which includes experience in other areas than music, in the long run makes for the better musician. I don't believe that was the attitude when I was a student. Too many things happen in life that make it impossible to continue on a course set by parents for a child at a very early age; there are too many unknowns, side roads, and often there are personal tragedies produced by an enforced obsession. And years ago, when I was starting out, there seemed many opportunities: there used to be two orchestras—CBS and NBC—flourishing on radio; theaters still had orchestras which were part of the Broadway world; the recording business was growing, thriving, and most of it was done in New York. So as a freelancer you could find work which paid well by doing recordings; you could make a little less but be a little more satisfied by doing concerts; you could make money doing jingles in the commercial world. Then these opportunities moved away from New York. Nowadays, with the kids, I try to be brutally frank. If they're not outstanding talents, I tell them, not only are you going to have a rough time, chances are you'll have a horrible time. And even if they are outstanding, there isn't that much choice.

Int.: When the choice presented itself to you—when you were invited to join the Beaux Arts Trio—what were the mechanics of transition?

I.C.: One day I got a call from Bernie and Menahem, asking would I join the Trio. Again it was a dream come true because I'd always admired them tremendously; I said of course I'd be glad, I'd be delighted to join. But we've got to get together and play and see how we match, I assume; it takes some time to uncover differences of opinion and approach. But they said, no, it's a question of your saying whether or not you want to join. And I found this astounding because when I joined the Juilliard, for example, we spent a couple of days together playing, working together to gauge the means of arriving at the musical ideas—whether that worked to our mutual advantage. But the Trio's approach wasn't like that. I knew Bernie from Juilliard; I didn't know Menahem at all, though I had heard the Trio often. They had heard me once, I remember, and came backstage—but that was it. So I was flabbergasted and said, by all means, that's great.

Int.: I remember having traveled with you on what was one of your first tours of Europe with the Trio—perhaps the first time you played together in Germany, in 1970. And you were working immensely hard, acquiring the repertoire.

I.C.: I've got news for you, Nick, I still am. But now for other reasons; now it becomes more elusive, the holding on to what you've got . . . .

Int.: So in the course of your career you've played with several ensembles, with orchestras, and on a free-lance basis. Is there a way in which your sense of commitment has altered over time, has become more focused—or are these several strings to the same bow?

I.C.: I believe I'm more vitally interested in the Trio than I was in the Quartet. Yet I've always felt that any kind of music making—whether you're playing as a soloist or as a member of an ensemble, any ensemble, or anonymously in an orchestra—in whatever the context the important thing is the music. And I get tremendous joy from a Beethoven symphony when I'm sitting in an orchestra—which, admittedly, I haven't done for a long time. The effort and practice has no relation to the ensemble as such, whether it be a trio or quartet or a symphony; I study the music with the same interest, curiosity, enjoyment. And even when I used to do free-lancing in New York—the jingles, the commercial work—I felt there was a knack to doing that well. I admired the good craftsmen. I always admired the guys, if I had to play a show, who had the technique for reading the thing and performing it right off. You know, there's a recording session with a conductor; you may have seen the music before or you may have not, you're not prepared, you don't know his idiosyncracies as a conductor, you're expected to sit down and record. And the ability to respond in such a circumstance is also craft. Very often the demands are extreme; some of the stuff is easy to play, of course, but they might put a sheet of music in front of you and say, this is the tempo, okay, let's go, one, two, three. The people who can just sit down and play are impressive; it's not something I'd look down on.

Int.: What were some of the processes of adjustment entailed by your entry to the Trio; what do you remember having focused on?

I.C.: There are differences when you play with strings only and when you're playing in a piano trio. For example, the piano note sounds as soon as the pianist depresses the key—but string players slide into a note. So there's a problem with initial attack, which is something one must conquer early on. There's the problem of intonation. The piano is supreme in that domain, because if it's in tune you can't quibble with it; even out of tune it's forever correct. But it's what we call a tempered pitch. String players tend to raise certain notes, to lower other notes for expressive reasons. We do this almost instinctively, depending on our feelings about the harmonic structure and function of a particular chord. But that can't be done in playing with the piano, or only to a tiny degree. There's an additional problem, having to to do with balance. The piano can be orchestral; again this depends on the pianist. Luckily our pianist is most sensitive—Menahem actually started out on the violin. The piano can drown us out completely if it so chooses; there's nothing we can do. I heard an amusing story about a teacher who was upset about the balance between violin and piano in a group he was coaching. And he said to the pianist, "Look, look, if you put a violin on top of a piano, nothing happens. But put the piano on top of the violin . . ." This image was so vivid the student burst into tears.

Int.: Did you feel that you were forging something new in the Trio—something that was, to a degree, at odds with their previous work?

I.C.: Any person joining a group which has been in existence for a while will feel successful if he can get across some of his ideas about musical interpretation. The members of the group will be bound to want to affect the new member, to shape him into the previous mold. So there is a constant interchange.

Int.: Did you listen to the old performances? You've been rerecording trios lately—the Beethoven cycle, for instance. Are you conscious of a pattern previously set together with Guilet, and was that a pattern to imitate or change?

I.C.: I'd heard the Trio, of course, in performance—but I don't listen to records because I want no preconceptions. I prefer, ideally, to study the score and come to my own conclusions. We hope to achieve something better, but it may not work out that way. When I was at Juilliard I was aware that many students, given a new piece, would immediately listen to a recording. And then they tried to imitate it; there's a great danger that way of losing your own individuality, of having it submerged. It's an interesting question because I've been associated with people who were great teachers as well as performers. And very often the strong teacher can have a bad effect on a student by virtue of the fact that he *is* so authoritative. I think a teacher should be afraid to dampen the feeling of creativity in a student; he can insist that you (1) do my fingering, (2) do my bowings, (3) do it musically the way I do it. And what's left for the student? There's no adequate preparation for the young artist who must eventually set out on his own. I've seen some remarkable talents who, when under the tutelage of a great teacher, were absolutely marvelous. But when it came to breaking out on their own, they were lost. . . . So the teacher should prepare the student for that moment when he does go out, when he leaves the teacher behind.

Int.: I take it you don't subscribe to the techniques of enforced, mechanical learning.

I.C.: If it is mere rote learning and mechanical efficiency, then no, I would not subscribe. But the Suzuki school, for example, was started by a man who considered music a way of helping with one stage of life. What I've heard of those young people in the Suzuki schools I admire greatly. There's a great reliance, for example, on the ear; they learn to play before they learn to read music. I was taught to play while learning to read music. We were recently in Japan, so I do know a little about their problem, and Western music does really present a problem to those ensembles we heard. I discussed this with a Japanese teacher. I went to some of their plays, the Noh theater, and Kabuki, and the intensity of expression—the variety and wealth of sound—is greater than what I have experienced in the Western world. So I asked him, "How come, when they do a Beethoven trio, they have neither sensitivity nor passion?" And he said, "We have a fear of expressing it, we don't have the conviction just to go ahead and cut loose, or display the emotion adequately in the music."

Int.: The Trio undertake new repertoire relatively seldom by now. Are you conscious, after these years of performing, of a certain regularity entailed by performance; is there a nightly or weekly alteration? And do you still argue over Ravel; how do the dynamics of presentation vary?

I.C.: Yes, we do. We still argue over Ravel, or Beethoven, or Mozart. I think perhaps we always will, and at the point we stop feeling strongly enough to argue over a phrase we'll have reached a sad point indeed. Brahms made a perceptive remark; he said, play new music as if it were classic, and classic as if it were new. And I've always felt, for a performer, that's an ideal objective. You must approach what has been done and done again with a freshness—as something which is new, daring, *bright* to you. But you must give a different impression with the new; if it *is* brand-new you should have digested it as if you've known the music all your life. I find something useful in that idea. I remember, once we were somewhere in Europe, waiting for a train, and we heard a Schumann trio on the radio. And we listened and said, that can't be us, you don't slide there, do you? not that way, the tempo isn't exactly right—but we said the performance itself was not bad. It turned out to be us.

We have a large repertoire. We don't limit our repertoire on tour and sometimes play thirty works on a two- or three-week trip; that's the equivalent of seven or eight different programs. And to keep that music in your head, in your heart, in the fingers is not easy; I don't care how many times you may have played this, it needs individual work before the group gets together, and then the group must rehearse. Yes, every evening is different. If we had to play the same work five nights in a row, there'd be differences on each of those five nights. There'd be tiny differences in tempo, in interpretation, the individual and net performances; I think we are sensitive to such things as the acoustics of the hall, the reaction you get from the audience—you may think they're bored or feel they're listening intently. And your own physical makeup varies. Sometimes you are more lyrical, sometimes a little bit impatient; sometimes you feel the music intensely, sometimes you are a bit withdrawn. These are things you cannot control. It really is a question of the inspiration of the moment, and I think we as a group honor inspiration. We don't look for a performance which is set and then try to reproduce it. I've played in groups where that *is* the objective. And I think that is neither possible nor desirable; the element of inspiration is something to be sought. That implies the same point of view on the part of those you play with; it also implies confidence in what you're doing, a willingness to take the chance. And I think we as an ensemble have that.

Int.: Could you talk a little about the performing life, the demands on your energy and time, the ways you maintain concentration on the road?

I.C.: The demands are extreme. I thought that as time went on they might diminish; they don't. If anything, they become greater. This has of course something to do with success. Or it may be a question of personality; maybe some people can relax about their performances. Time seems less and less available; there's more pressure to attend social affairs. Travel can be exhausting. You would think that sitting three, four, five, six hours at a time can be relaxing, and you would emerge from the airplane refreshed; it doesn't work that way. Delays of course can be catastrophic. But on the other hand, there's a certain momentum which comes from performance—and this is lacking if you perform rarely. I've found that sometimes, even though there are stresses and you don't have the time to practice or prepare the way you should, just the business of performing day after day has a kind of momentum and gets you through.

Int.: Do you feel there's a one-to-one correspondence between your sense of how a performance went and the audience reaction? Does this hold true of the critics' response also?

I.C.: I think we pride ourselves on a rapport with the audience—but there *are* those occasions when you thought, ah, that was marvelous, we enjoyed ourselves tremendously. But the audience did not. Or you thought it was good, but the critics said otherwise. Some critic will say the audience enjoyed itself, but he did not . . .

Int.: You routinely rehearse or try out a hall before a concert?

I.C.: It's not so much a question of conscientiousness as of necessity. Each evening the piano is a different instrument. So of course we must rehearse.

Int.: In that regard the piano is the variable, is it not? You spoke earlier of the piano as a standard against which the string instruments must measure themselves—to which they adjust. Yet it becomes the thing that alters—mechanically speaking—night to night.

I.C.: All sorts of things can happen. Suddenly a note can refuse to sound, strings can break, pedals can fall off or misfunction. We had a beautiful scene not long ago; we were doing the Ravel, and Menahem is in one of those runs in the first movement—and suddenly the sound just doesn't go away, it keeps building up and up. We looked at him as if to say, *messhugener*, what are you doing?; you know, get off the pedal. He shrugs his shoulders, and finally we had to stop because the sustaining pedal was just stuck. We tried to do something with the pedal, but there was nothing to do. The piano tuner will often stay backstage through the performance in case anything happens—but this particular guy was busy, I suppose, and he went off; he thought he had finished his job for the night. We then asked the audience if there was anybody who happened to be a piano tuner—"Is there a *Klavierstimmer* in the house?" No. Well, Bernie has fiddled around a little with these things, so there was the picture of Bernie down on his knees, his rear facing the audience, tails flapping, trying to get the pedal to work. We tried that for around ten minutes, and then we called an intermission, wondering what to do. And luckily a man came up and said he had once been a piano tuner and he'd try to fix it. He did.

Int.: What of your own instrument? What are its properties, and how did you acquire it?

I.C.: My first Strad was loaned to me through Alexander Schneider—or Sascha, as everyone calls him. He got me the Baron Gutman Strad when we were playing together in the Schneider Quartet—and that was a beautiful fiddle. It had a thick, buttery sound. After our project was over, I had to return the instrument, so I started looking around for a good one for myself. I could find nothing to satisfy me, but in the meantime Sascha wanted to acquire a Guarnerius which had come up for sale. He had always had a Strad, and I said to him one day almost flippantly, "Look, why don't I buy your Strad and then you use the money to buy the Guarnerius?" He said, "Okay," just like that. This would have been the late fifties. I didn't have enough money to buy the instrument, so I gambled on the stock market. A friend of ours was a nurse in a hospital. A very famous financier with a reputation as a miser was there as a patient; instead of giving the nurses cash, he gave them tips on the market. She came back one day and said, "Guess what he told me, he said buy this and this." By God, I took every penny I had, and I bought this and this. I also got my parents to buy this and this. And this and this panned out.

Sascha was very kind and sweet and decent. I paid for the instrument what he had paid for it ten or fifteen years earlier. He would not take a penny above what he paid, and I'm sure the instrument had appreciated at least a hundred percent.

Int.: What is its name?

I.C.: The "Brodsky," made in 1702, at the beginning of the so-called "long period" of Stradivarius. Sascha used to play it in the Budapest Quartet. It's a very fine instrument—a good, strong, healthy instrument; it's not one of the great Strads, but neither is it a poor one. I don't think any violinist is completely overjoyed with the instrument he has. At first it's a love affair, but then you realize that the instrument, just like a person, has certain limitations. And we're never sure whether the limitations are ours or the instrument's; I've always assumed that they're mine. I think it's a healthier approach. Some people are always adjusting parts of the instrument—the bridge, the sound post. I feel, no, it's up to me to adjust to the weather, the change of seasons. . . .

Int.: How does such a process of adjustment relate—if at all—to the recording situation? You have spoken repeatedly of the willingness to adapt, of the variety and responsiveness appropriate to performance. Yet a recording is fixed.

I.C.: Yes. It's a different proposition, and the problem in recording is to try to play as if there were an audience. It mustn't be an artificial environment—yet this gadget they stick in front of us that takes down every little squeak inhibits us. So we have to try to get away from it, this feeling of being forever imprisoned by a mechanical device. Instead we must express ourselves. What happens in a recording is that one looks for a kind of technical perfection because the standards are so high. But does one get the musical values; are those transmitted, transferred? They are very elusive to get down on a machine. The mike makes you aware of every little problem, whether it be the squeak, the intonation, or the rhythm which isn't absolutely accurate. One becomes preoccupied. And the danger is that one becomes obsessed with technical concerns, whereas one should be concerned with musical values.

Int.: Would you say that the subordination of the individual to the ensemble is a prerequisite for chamber music making? There are of course greatly accomplished soloists who perform with great éclat, but it sometimes seems to be almost a problem in post-Euclidean geometry; how measure the whole by the parts?

I.C.: The problem with the three marvelous soloists getting together for chamber music is that they don't stay together long enough. . . . It takes devotion. You must practice so intensively on the repertoire that it becomes the most important aspect of music making. There have been trios with marvelous personnel but with divided loyalties—so that they couldn't say, yes, here I make my principal commitment, this is my principal craft; here I define my career. That's what we have done, and it makes some difference, I think.

Int.: Can you amplify on that distinction—both in personal terms and for the Trio as a whole?

I.C.: Let me put it this way. The solo repertoire consists of a lot of music whose qualities may be subject to debate; a good deal of the repertoire consists of music which I do not respect purely as music. I will listen to a violinist who will play beautifully, and I'll say, isn't that remarkable, the double-stops, the fast passages, how great that is. But I sometimes think that the music is junk—and here's a man who takes this junk and makes a great performance. So I respect the performance, I admire what the man has done. But I started late on the instrument; my interest did not focus on this kind of music. A Beethoven string quartet or trio is more appealing to me than a Paganini concerto. To me, the former is the more demanding; it asks more of the artist, of the serious musician. However the Paganini does require extreme facility; there's no question about it. Perhaps it's because I never had the facility that I knew where my path lay.

In terms of the Trio, what matters in this regard is that we have persisted. That is a distinction. It takes persistence to make yourself known to the musical world, to stick together so that the repertoire becomes a part of you, to make adjustments for personality. And there aren't going to be three angels who get along, because three angels will not necessarily make for an exciting ensemble. There must be some disagreement, some discussion as to why it *has* to be played that way. Because through the conflict and during the discussion something emerges, something additional is born. But most groups, I think, flounder because of personal relationships which deteriorate. Then the personal carries over into the musical, and you fail to function together on a musical level. Then the ensemble disbands.

Int.: How does this personal animus—trust or animosity, even—make itself current in musical terms? Do you ever feel tempted to say, after a rehearsal, they're wrong, they're being unreasonable, this is how it should sound and how I'm going to play.

I.C.: Indeed, that's a danger. When it gets to the point where you say, they're fools, *I've* got the whole story, it takes that little bit of the angel in you to say, well, maybe I'm wrong. Or to agree on a trade-off: to say, let's do it once your way and then once in mine. There must be that skepticism about one's own strong conviction that says, ah, in the long run maybe it's best that I do what the majority says. One rarely admits that one is also a possible fool. . . . When that does take place—when you say, I'll give up this thing I feel so strongly about—it is sensed by the others, appreciated. I think also some of us say in rehearsal, no, no, I'm not going to do it like that, and then in the performance you say, all right, I'll do it, the problem must be solved. It does take that kind of self-sacrifice, and that's really just a question of negating the personal ego—of being willing to continue the search for a shared conception.

Int.: How do you adjudicate this willingness to change—this desire to remain free of the metronomically fixed repetitions of a recording—with the need not to surprise your colleagues in performance? How much interpretative latitude, beyond that agreed on in rehearsal, do you permit yourself?

Int.: One is not set in a mold by the music; one can do things on the spur of the moment. This sensitivity to appreciate a change in someone else's concept is an attitude to strive for. In other words, I will treasure what might happen momentarily, unexpectedly, because I think that sometimes—not always—something may emerge which approaches what we call, in quotes, "the truth." There's a great deal of instinct involved. Now sometimes it may be completely wrong, out of proportion; it may be in bad taste. Still, I think the three of us do feel that as an integrated part of music making. The other part is being sure enough of oneself to be willing to take a chance, to diverge from what was the set pattern—to be willing to say, okay, for the moment it's this, let's see what will happen.

Further, there are rare moments in music when

one feels a little bit taken out of oneself, and if these moments survive without being disturbed by somebody else—somebody who says, what's this, we never discussed that, how dare you attempt it!—that rapport is rare and precious and what we're looking for. I remember once we played all the Beethoven Trios in Divonne-les-Bains, and Josef Szigeti came to each of the concerts; each evening he came backstage. He had great knowledge of the repertoire, and he said, "This and this bowing in this and this passage, you know, that was written for a particular violinist."

Then he said, "You know, sometimes a composer asks you to do things which are too difficult, which you don't feel you can do. Should you then give in to your weakness and accomplish this task in some other way?" I said, "Well, yes, if I just can't do it that way." Szigeti said, "I know what you mean, but sometimes it might work, maybe once in five or ten." So I said, "What about all the other times?" And he said, "Ah, but think of that one time!"

Int.: Can you amplify on that open-ended term you used, "bad taste"?

I.C.: There is no such thing; it's too vague. I suppose I should have said "style." We each believe we know the styles of, let's say, German music, French music, Russian music. If one plays Russian music the way one plays Fauré, you would say, well, that isn't the right style; if a vibrato seems excessive in a certain repertoire—Bach, for instance—then you have the feeling that the music stylistically isn't correct. If one is not playing the romantic repertoire but is using all sorts of romantic slides, then you say, that's excessive, that's not valid. On the other hand, it doesn't mean the baroque repertoire can't accommodate slides; it has to do perhaps with the way the slide is done, its purpose. Is it an expressive slide or a slide of convenience that helps you get from one note to the other in a certain spot? Good style is hard to define. On the other hand, it's quite obvious when you hear a French-trained violinist playing the French repertoire—Francescatti, for instance, or Daniel Guilet. It's a sensitivity: the use of a certain vibrato, the use of the bow. . . . In playing for contemporary composers, I've always felt that the ones I respected were not inflexible about what you did to their music. They permitted a certain degree of freedom. I've found that the lesser composers were the ones who insisted, no, I said *mezzo piano* and that's not my conception of *mezzo piano*. I think the great composers believe their work will endure even if one does not adhere to the exact indications of the music.

Int.: If you were consigned by a malign conductor to perform the work of only one composer forever after, is there one composer you'd feel willing to select?

I.C.: No. It's impossible, because there are too many—luckily, too many—great works I can enjoy. Here at Marlboro I just recently read through a quartet of Haydn—Opus 20, Number 5, in F Minor. What beauty of expression: the first movement is Schubert, the slow movement is Beethoven, the Minuet-Scherzo has that peasant quality you often find in Haydn, the last movement's a fugue. There's the Haydn of the elegant court, there's Haydn the Gypsy—he was born in a Gypsy area—there's the man of classic purity and the man of earthy, gutsy qualities at the same time. . . . Then I do a quintet, a two-viola quintet of Mozart; I say to myself, my God, what sheer natural beauty, what joy! Then you come to the sublime Beethoven. I can only say, with me, it's a favorite for a week, maybe a month or a couple of months; I would hate to have to make a choice.

Int.: You don't, I take it, regret having failed to pursue a career as a doctor?

I.C.: No. When you have the privilege of interpreting this great art, which is not just sensual but philosophical—when, as in a Beethoven slow movement sometimes, you are taken out of yourself, one with whatever it is you believe in—and can bring pleasure to others as well, that is supremely gratifying. I still get that electric shock, still whistle in the morning the tune I played last night. I remember I used to say, with wonder, my God, they pay you for this. . . .

But you cannot put life temporarily aside, or push it away and spend all your time in music. Because then I think you will not be able to appreciate, to understand, to be able to feel what the great composers—those superb human beings—were after. And there are those rare geniuses who were abysmal people—prejudiced, selfish, bigots—but still were great creative artists. But perhaps to understand that requires knowledge of human nature also. And then I remember what a colleague once said at Juilliard, "More important than music is life."

Greenhouse, Pressler, and Daniel Guilet at the airport
(KLM Royal Dutch Airlines Photo)

Guilet, Pressler, and Greenhouse in rehearsal with Aaron Copland at Tanglewood
(Whitestone Photo)

Pressler with the Philadelphia Orchestra, 1947

Greenhouse in the early 1950s

Pressler, with Darius Milhaud, after winning the Debussy Competition in San Francisco, 1946 (Ben Greenhaus)

The Beaux Arts Trio
with Toscanini

The Trio with Pablo
Casals in Puerto
Rico, 1958

Isidore Cohen and Leonard Bernstein confer during Juilliard Quartet recording of Schumann Piano Quintet.

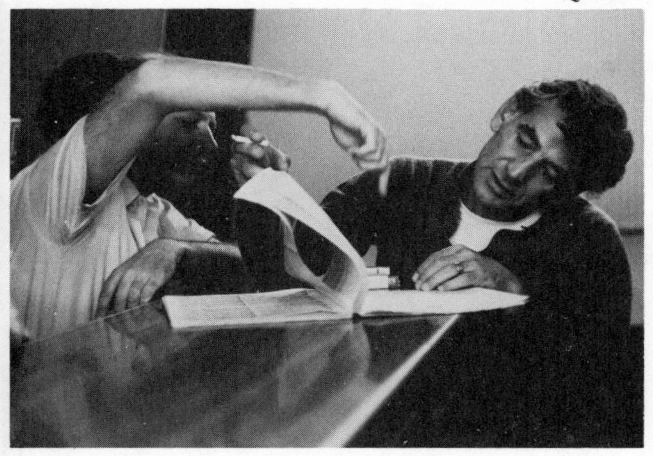

With Igor Stravinsky

Isaac Stern receives an award from Mayor Ed Koch of New York, 1982. From left to right: Felix Galimir, Michael Tree, Julius Levine, Koch, Stern, Isidore Cohen, and Alexander Schneider (Holland Wemple)

Greenhouse and Bruno Giuranna at La Chaux-de-Fonds, 1983
(Nicholas Delbanco)

The crew from Philips Records at the entrance to Théâtre Musica. Robert Ritscher, Willem Van Leeuwen, and Volker Straus, left to right
(Nicholas Delbanco)

The Trio recording Beethoven's Triple Concerto, 1977, with Bernard Haitink on the podium and Volker Straus at the microphones
(Mike Evans)

Backstage at the Brooklyn Academy of Music, 1981. Presentor Scott Nickrenz is visible in mirror. (Allen Cohen)

A Philips Records publicity photo

Greenhouse at B.A.M. (Allen Cohen)

Chapter Five

The Trio take recording seriously. They travel at least twice a year to a small town in Switzerland, La Chaux-de-Fonds. In the foothills of the Jura Mountains, thirteen kilometers from the French border, La Chaux was once a center of the Swiss watchmaking industry. It has a horological museum to commemorate the "art of time," and a Musée de Beaux Arts—but it is scarcely a tourist center or a traveler's delight. The men come there to work. They do so with a concentrated intensity and with the techniques of rehearsal rather than performance; they play an empty hall. At the start of their career, they subsidized the cost of a recording; now there is a crew in attendance. These pages will describe, in detail, one recording period: January 6 to 12, 1983.

We meet at the Hôtel Moreau. I have taken a plane from Madrid and a train from Geneva to Lausanne, changed at Neuchâtel, and then taken the local for La Chaux-de-Fonds. The trip is uneventful but prolonged; I reach the hotel at nine-thirty at night. The desk clerk informs me that the "musicals" are already here and have gone to "exercise" at the concert hall. They arrive in the lobby at a quarter past ten. They have come from separate starting points and are more than a little weary: Greenhouse and Cohen, arriving from New York, were collected at the airport and driven to these foothills from Geneva. Pressler has come from Tel Aviv, where he spent the holidays teaching. And Bruno Giuranna, a fourth artist, has arrived from Rome. He was to have met Pressler in Zurich and they had planned to travel together; fog delayed Giuranna, however, and he had to take the train. Giuranna knows the Trio, but not well. They are to record the Mozart G Minor Piano Quartet, K. 478, and the E-flat Piano Quartet, K. 493. (By now, the Beaux Arts have recorded the bulk of the trio literature, and they are branching out to piano quartets, quintets, and the like). Since this is relatively unfamiliar repertoire, and they have not joined forces with this violist often before, they have budgeted a full five days—January 7 through 12—for a single record. "When we paid for our recording time," Greenhouse recalls, "way back when we started and did the Beethoven series, we produced the whole edition in five days. . . ."

Giuranna lives in Rome. He is a compact, handsome man with wavy hair, white at the temples, a ready smile, much charm. A founding member of I Musici, he has played with the Quartetto di Roma and now the Trio Italiano d'Archi; he has taught at the Accademia Chigiana in Siena, at Detmold and Berlin. He wants to simplify his life, he tells me, and teach only at Berlin. He plans to make his home about fifty kilometers north of Venice, in a house he has renovated in Asolo. "It's a hill village," he says. "Your poet Robert Browning made it popular. He used the word *asolando,* meaning 'go for a stroll in the hills.' Imagine. As if we said, when we go to the city, 'New Yorking.' But"—he spreads his hands, evoking vistas, cobbled streets—"I love it there. You will, too."

We have a late, cold supper in the hotel restaurant; the waiter does what he can, this side of impoliteness, to indicate he'd like to go home. It is midnight when he leaves. There has been desultory chat of politics and weather and who has played with whom; they are satisfied with the test levels established that evening. Outside, a chill rain thickens into snow.

* * *

Recording is an indispensable component part of a career. Records (and cassettes) remain the medium by which a majority of performers reach the majority of their audience—providing, of course, that they make records at all. The stage and studio, if not two sides of the same coin, nonetheless share a currency. A single widely broadcast performance of, say, the Beethoven Triple Concerto will be heard by a larger public than would attend an entire concert season; the audience at home dwarfs those who go to the hall.

Put it another way: it's possible to imagine an avid chamber music enthusiast who has never managed to attend a live performance; reasons of geography or health or limited time or funds could well keep him away. Yet the reverse is not the case: those who come to concerts will without exception have a hall at home. They can select their own programs; they can hear the retired or dead. A performer—witness Glenn Gould—can sustain a reputation and enlarge an audience while refusing to "perform." The equipment may be outmoded or chic, inexpensive, or elaborate—but a shelf of records is the sine qua non of the music lover, and the single best index of taste.

For the contemporary concert artist, records represent a kind of legacy. The dancer cannot pattern his technique on that of Nijinsky, nor the cellist on that of Boccherini—since those legendary performers are but the stuff of legend once their performance is done. They antedate the apparatus of retention—tape and film. But the tenor Hugues Cuenod when old can hear Cuenod when young, and the serious student of an instrument can learn from his masters at home. Further, and increasingly, the microphone's ear is exact. It makes no concession to bonhomie or the occasion's excitement; it has had no wine with dinner and is seated next to no inamorata for the night. Once it records an error, that error will remain. In the heat of performance, a missed note or muffled passage need not matter; if noticed at all, it is noted once only, and the performers move on. So a record can attain a precision not present onstage and an exacting accuracy that nears the absolute. Technological advance has been both rapid and real. Thomas Edison heard nothing like the sound available today; what we call "high fidelity" will no doubt seem archaic to the listener twenty years hence. Already the laser replaces the needle, and cassettes orbit the earth in satellites for the benefit of future intergalactic fans.

Those who own a record of the Beaux Arts Trio performance, or have heard them on the radio, may be more likely to buy a ticket when the Trio come to town. The young musician who has paid for his first album hopes to hawk signed copies onstage after he performs—and the Trio, too, can be prevailed upon to sit in the lobby and sell. Record outlets stock the disks of those who appear in the region; if a performer is popular in Sweden or in Italy, the chances are that he has performed there of late. Conversely, sales representatives can tell by slumping sales figures that their artist has not been, in recent memory, around. Absence breeds commercial failure as often as presence success.

The Trio record exclusively for Philips Records, and has since the beginning (the three exceptions to that rule are here appended in the Discography). In the late fifties they made a test pressing, at their own expense, of Beethoven's *Archduke* Trio and sent it to a friend of Greenhouse's in Austria, Kurt Liszt. He submitted it to a small label,

Amadeo Records, but—with what turns out in retrospect to have been characteristic good fortune—the sample was refused. Liszt then submitted the record to personnel at Philips, who asked to hear a version of the *Geister* Trio also. This was accepted, and they proceeded to record (with Daniel Guilet) the complete Piano Trios of Beethoven. Success attended these early efforts, and the contract has been fruitful for both sides. By now the musicians have received every major recording award, from the Grammy to the Prix d'Honneur du Prix Mondial du Disque de Montreux to the Deutsche Schallplattenpreis. Philips, a branch of Phonogram International—other branches include such labels as Decca Records and Deutsche Grammophon—has its headquarters in Amsterdam; it is a Dutch company, and large. Philips has sent its personnel and equipment to La Chaux-de-Fonds and reserved the Théâtre Musica for a week; the company is responsive, clearly, to the quantity of records the Trio make and sell.

At eleven o'clock on the morning of January 7, the musicians gather at the concert hall. It is a brief walk from the hotel. The streets are clean, but the sidewalk has high-heaped snow. "We expected a meter," the hotel clerk says. "It's very good weather today." The Philips crew, too, stay at the hotel; they have arrived two days before and readied the recording studio—a converted cloakroom at the entry level of the theater, on the left. The producer, Volker Straus, has been working with the Trio for twelve years. Born in Germany, he has lived near Amsterdam and been employed by Philips since 1959. "I came on April first," he says. "Exactly half my life ago. It was an April Fool's joke." He is a lean man with the protuberant belly of someone who fails to get sufficient exercise; he has, the musicians assure me, excellent ears. His eyes are deeply recessed, his face lined. His hair is brown and wavy; at breakfast he appears meticulous, but as the day wears on he will grow shaggy, intent.

The piano tuner comes from Hanover. Robert Ritscher—his card reads "*Klaviertechniker und Stimmer*"—is six feet two, fifty years old. He does gymnastics, he tells me; he has an excellent constitution and a new, young wife. While Straus orders eggs and orange juice and croissants for breakfast, Ritscher confines himself to coffee; his wife has insisted he must return—he pats his stomach—thin. Straus calls him the best piano tuner they have. "Maybe there's a better one in Mongolia," he says. "But this side of Mongolia, no." Ritscher fakes embarrassment; he cackles and shrugs. Then he produces a newspaper article on Hermann der Cherusker, that memorialized German warrior who drove the Romans back south. He waves the photograph at Giuranna, saying, "Do you recognize this?"

Giuranna laughs. He, too, records for Philips and has met Ritscher before. "They think it's their heroics," he says. "But it was the weather. The weather and the food. Every Roman soldier wanted to go home. You can keep your Detmold, friend."

The third member of the crew, Willem van Leeuwen, is the recording engineer. "I've worked for Philips since '53," he says. "I'll stay till they retire me, I guess." He makes an upward motion, pointing his thumb at the ceiling. He has thick white hair, a round, clear face; he wears glasses and a short-sleeved blue shirt. There is an air of camaraderie, of competence throughout. The musicians assemble onstage. Pressler has been practicing since nine. He has performed these pieces only rarely. "It's a piano concerto," he says. "I have to treat it that way, I have to catch up." Greenhouse, on the other hand, is unconcerned; he has not even brought the music with him from New York. Straus presents him with the score. "It's a continuo part, more or less," Greenhouse says. "I imitate the piano's left hand. Mozart made it easy on cellists." And Giuranna knows the literature by heart; it is a staple of his repertoire. He approaches Pressler and picks out—on the viola—the next piano phrase. "*Ach, das ist eine Schweinerei,*" Pressler says. "That's awful; you know it too well."

Conversation is, as so often in Europe and routinely in Switzerland, a linguistic muddle. Straus and Van Leeuwen speak together in Dutch and to Ritscher in German; they weave in English at will. "Yes, my dear," Van Leeuwen says, when Straus asks, is he ready. French is the language of La Chaux-de-Fonds; Giuranna, an Italian, addresses the chambermaids in Spanish; Yiddish expressions, too, enter in. "*Ich habe quasi improvisatore ici,*" is the sort of thing one hears, and gesture must complement meaning. The musicians refer to a "vedge," and I ask them what that means. "Nail," says Giuranna, offering the Italian term, "that's what we call it anyway." "Not an accent?" I inquire. "Haven't you heard of the Vizard of Oz?" Pressler asks, and then he spells it—"w-e-d-g-e."

This leads to a discussion of markings, and how Mozart composed almost without them. On the verge of paranoia in his later years, and in fear of having his compositions stolen, he used a kind of shorthand to sketch in the theme. "It's remarkable," says Pressler. "In his lifetime just three things were published. And the *Dissonant* Quartet, for instance, when they played it for some Count, he said to the musicians, 'how come you play so many wrong notes?' They said, 'This is how it's written, Excellency.' And then he tore it up!"

* * *

The microphones are already in place, and the chairs. Van Leeuwen bustles about the players as they assume their seats; he cuts and places strips of tape to indicate the chairs' positionings. If they move two inches on the floor, or a microphone is jostled, the balance will shift. "You can tape my foot," says Greenhouse. "I won't move, I promise." Each artist has a standing mike in front of him with twin receivers; three rows back in the auditorium proper, there are two fifteen-foot mikes. In front of the stage, ten feet high, stands a column with a red and a green bulb at the top. The green light is turned on to indicate recording is in process, the red light that it has stopped.

The control room is three flights down; black wire cables snake up the stairs. I ask why Philips, based in Amsterdam, cuts its records here in Switzerland. Straus offers several reasons. "We have uninterrupted use of the Musica Théâtre," he says. "But at home, in the Concertgebouw, we have to make way for orchestra rehearsals and performance. Here we can rent the whole hall. It's cheaper, you see, and not so much traffic noise. For a chamber music session we must turn the microphone levels high—less so for an orchestra. And therefore if there's street noise, we'd pick it up. In 1967, I was with Gérard Souzay, and he said, there's a wonderful hall in La Chaux, do you know it? So we came to listen and I've been coming since."

The four musicians warm up. They run through the movement "for levels"; Straus has turned on the green light. After the first run-through, he will invite them to listen. There are false starts. "I'd like a little less activity on that bu-bu-bu-bu," says Cohen. He sings the phrase. "For me," says Pressler, "it's the bush that burns underneath." Three bars later, Cohen stops again; "I have a request. If you would slow here for my fingering?" Giuranna nods, then turns to Greenhouse. "I'd be happy to follow the cello. But a little less excited." "Shall we go on?" Pressler says.

For the next five days, this scene will be repeated. It will be played several ways. For the most part there's good humor—a smattering of jokes, as when Greenhouse and Giuranna trade bows, or when Greenhouse caresses the neck of the cello as if it were a woman's. Each of them sings. Often they talk all at once. "Has it ever happened," Giuranna asks, "that you had a mosquito in a recording session?" Greenhouse, who sits smoking in rehearsal, flicks the ash from his cigar. "With this thing? Not a chance."

"Let's play from V," Cohen says. "V?" "Yes, V as in Victor." "As in V.D." "As in Vee shall see," says Pressler. "Let's start the bar before," says Greenhouse. "Oh," says Giuranna, relieved. "I'm reading triplets. But I understood the bottom four. Not the bar before."

At other moments, they argue. "That sounds *vermisht,*" says Pressler. "I didn't hear that." "What's wrong with your ears?" says Greenhouse. "I play what's written."

"But I didn't hear it."

"Whatever you don't hear isn't there; you'll have to talk to Mozart."

"I hope to someday," Pressler says. "Only don't hurry me, please."

Greenhouse persists. "Why can't I keep a tempo? I can't follow if you push the run."

"I'm sorry, it's *my* run. You come in inexact."

"Don't get fixated on it." Cohen intercedes: "We'll bring a metronome."

Pressler yields. "All right. I'll practice with the metronome an hour after lunch."

Approval is taken for granted; disagreement must be

spelled out. Professionals, they won't waste time with praise.

The facilities at Théâtre Musica are old. There is no observation bubble behind which engineers survey their subjects; the studio is catercorner to the bathroom and lined with two rows of hooks. A recording console sits in the room's center; two electrostatic loudspeakers form the base of an equilateral triangle, its apex at Straus's chair. Behind him sits Van Leeuwen with two tape decks in simultaneous operation: an analogue and a digital. The final record will derive from the digital recorder, but those tapes will be returned untouched to Amsterdam for processing; the analogue system, Van Leeuwen explains, is quicker to work with (when they need to retrieve a passage) and doubles as a backup in case the digital fails. The console contains an eight-track system, of which they use two: the violin and piano are on one track, the viola and cello on another. Additional equipment—a third speaker, in case of malfunction, boxes of tools, and wire and tape—waits piled up on a refectory table. Straus and Van Leeuwen have come here by truck; they will dismantle the equipment after this session is done.

The stage feels cold. The musicians wear sweaters—Giuranna, Cohen, and Greenhouse in brown, Pressler, blue. Except for stage lights, the hall is dark. Its size is moderate—twenty-seven rows with thirty-seven seats per row, and a narrow balcony; the curtains are drawn. Organ pipes span stage rear. A video camera, its red eye unwinking, establishes contact between the two floors; Straus rarely consults it, however. He uses a portable phone. When he needs to talk to the players above, he presses the buzzer; the second phone stands by the piano, and Pressler responds. They exchange readings. "The intonation in bars 108 through 110 is not quite right," says Straus. "The B flat is a bit flat in 184." Greenhouse asks about bars 190 through 194, and he says, "Yes, 194 was a bit out of tune; in 207 you rush a bit; in 299 the trill is not in time. Then"—to Pressler again—"in 315 it's absolutely in time, but it sounds a bit rushed."

Pressler loses his beloved pencil, it appears. He has brought it with him from Jerusalem; he mourns it, praising the eraser and the lead. The musicians all join the hunt; he requires this particular pencil to mark the score; it was just the right length, he insists. They produce alternative pencils. "No," Pressler says. "Mine was black." After fifteen minutes of searching, he finds it on the piano—in his score. The others tease him unmercifully; the pencil becomes a refrain. "Where's your pencil, Menahem?" they will ask at lunch, at dinner, in the street. "You could make a profit," Cohen says. "Buy the pencils for twenty-five cents and charge your students thirty-five, Menahem, it's a business." "The students come and take them," Pressler says. "So give those students who steal your pencils an A," Greenhouse suggests. "Graduate them quickly. And keep the ones who don't steal pencils in your class for years."

Conversation is technical, abrupt. "You stick to your bowing, I'll change mine." "Your resolution is our first note; give it to me a little clearer, please." "The first five notes after the slurred note, could you start a little lighter? It should sing." "So, let's try it from D." "Did you play a wrong note?" "I certainly did." "Where do you put the accent on this phrase, where do you want it?" "On the downbeat." "Then be careful of the A flat."

Their goal this Friday is the first movement of the E flat, with repeats. Giuranna has played the quartet as recently as ten days earlier, with friends. But there are adjustments to make: they compare bowings, fingering, tempi. When the green semaphore is on, the musicians perform. They joke about the time elapsed after a take. If Straus gets on the telephone immediately, he will have praise; if he takes three seconds, it's all right; if he takes longer, the suggestions accumulate. From time to time, he turns off the green light in the middle of a passage, and the men will sit onstage as if rebuffed. It is an arduous process; the first movement, lasting fourteen minutes, takes five hours to record. They produce twenty-three takes. Of these, two or three are full run-throughs; more often they will play agreed-on sections of the movement, and sometimes just a few bars. I ask Straus to explain this; shouldn't a recording strive for the feel of performance, and doesn't his machinery undermine the music's continuity?

"Yes," he says. "Of course." But he and Van Leeuwen share a distaste for "live recording"; there are too many mistakes. "In a performance," he says, "it's fine, because you just have to listen once. But if you have a record you can hear it many times, and even the deaf man can hear."

He sits at the console, marking the score. If a tempo is inexact, an intonation slightly shaded, a *forte* one beat too early, Straus reacts. He waves his pencil as might a conductor, breaking the rhythm to mark notes. He writes on top of the line if the interpretation pleased him, beneath it if not; he speaks to himself or nods or shakes his head; he mutters over his shoulder in Dutch. Van Leeuwen, too, keeps a recording log; he registers the number of takes, their length to the second, their position on the tape. He can therefore locate the successful or offending passage later, at Straus's request. Their stated intention is to be as neutral as possible, to distort sound as little as possible; Straus calls the console his hammer and screwdriver, the tool of his trade. "But when a piece of furniture is finished," he says, "you don't want to see any marks."

Onstage, the dialogue continues. "You know," says Cohen, "I feel that whenever we have the figure in unison"—he sings the phrase—"it lacks a drive, a sting; we have to feel what we're after, some emphasis perhaps." "I'm not sure it should sound like an echo," Pressler says. "I thought I replied to him," says Cohen. "Yes, but it's weaker, it's passive." Straus offers notes. "Not too much emphasis on the B flat; excellent, bars 99 to 100. Bar 125, you go back after your trill, but the strings are making an accent. Now the strings are too cautious perhaps." Every twenty minutes, eschewing the telephone and for the sake of variety, he carries his notes onstage. "I would like to have, between the F and the E, a kind of cello change. What's disturbing is the free A flat. The violin and viola are not together in bars 22 and 23; excuse me, it's a bit rushed."

Giuranna is lighthearted. "I don't understand," he says, "why the violin is considered such an important instrument; it should have been written for the viola." "What about the piano?" Pressler asks. "The piano," says Giuranna. "It doesn't even count." "Where is my pencil?" Pressler pats his pockets. He turns to Giuranna. "You took it, *gonif.*" Giuranna spreads his hands.

Downstairs, Straus begins to tire. "This *verdammte* first session," he says. "We should always start a record with the second session." At 6:45, they break for coffee. Robert Ritscher returns to the piano. He also is exacting; he has spent more than two hundred hours on this instrument. "Slowly, slowly," Ritscher says, "it has found its voice. One day it isn't there, and then suddenly it sings."

They finish at nine-fifteen. More than twelve hours earlier, Pressler had entered the hall. The attention to detail has been prodigious, but the time spent on generalities next to nonexistent. I ask Giuranna about this, since in his case the Trio's language is new. He cannot take for granted, as do they, a commonality of purpose, a shared interpretative approach. "They are musicians," he says. "I believe I am one, too. When musicians must discuss the piece, it's a very bad sign. You should have it in your head, of course, have considered it all in your head—but you must play with your heart." Straus would not have put it this way, but he agrees. "In Mozart," he says, "there's no room. You're either right or not right, there's absolutely no margin. Even in Beethoven or Schubert one has room—but here it is clear or unclear."

We have a late dinner at the Restaurant Elite. The musicians talk of who's performing where and whose health is how; it sounds less like gossip than a kind of catching up. They tell stories. A famous conductor was so drunk on the podium he had to be told, afterward, which piece he had conducted. A violinist joined a string quartet and told them—just as they were leaving for Japan—that he refused to fly. He had a phobia. They had to cancel the concert, but kept him in the group. They comment on Straus's taskmasterly precision; their grumbling is praise. "Most people can't hear," Greenhouse says. "They are technicians, not musicians. Like those television producers who focus on the oboe during a flute solo. Or who think a flute's a flute. But a flute in Mozart is completely different from a flute in Debussy."

Giuranna apologizes for having practiced in his room during the afternoon break; he was trying out new fingerings for the Paganini, and it must have sounded infernal. They assure him they couldn't hear it clearly and therefore it hadn't been bad. Cohen, too, has practiced in his room, and I tell him to use a stronger mute because his noise disturbs the rhythm of my typewriter. For an instant he takes me seriously. Greenhouse has been bothered by the altitude and the sharp cold of La Chaux; walking back to the hotel, he fights for breath. They bid each other goodnight and retire; soon, music emanates from their four adjacent rooms on the second floor. They each have turned on their radios. In the morning they will praise and damn the performance heard. In the morning I breakfast with Straus. He wears glasses in order to see; the hot milk for his coffee is rancid. He neither smells nor tastes it till the second cup; I observe that, for a man with such ears, his sense of smell and taste leave something to be desired. "Yes, it's what my wife says also." The milk is replaced.

The second session is productive, less constrained. They rehearse at eleven, starting with the third movement; if there is time that afternoon, they will record the second. The order of performing has been dictated by the degree of difficulty, and in reverse; the slow movement seems comparatively simple to perform. Again, conversation is polyglot and truncate: a spurt of suggestions. "Don't you think it would make it clear to me," says Greenhouse, "if the downbeat had some emphasis. A little bit of accentuation." "I play it towards you," Pressler says. "So, let's try from D." Ritscher enters and takes a front-row seat. "*Hier ist das Publikum.* Here is the public," he says.

When they assemble in the control room to listen to the takes, Straus positions them in front of their own tracks. The sound in the recording studio is drier than that in the hall. "It sounds too aggressive," says Cohen. "What's disturbing is the free A flat; that high note sounds piercing." "It's *nicht gut,*" whispers Van Leeuwen. "It's march music."

Often the scores disagree. Different editions have different markings, and the four of them can spend five minutes adjudicating a phrase. "What I have against this," Greenhouse says, "is it seems too dramatic, too precious. This thick unison." Pressler demurs. "It's mannered," Greenhouse says. "If you want to know what I really think, I think it's mannered." Again they play for hours under the imperious green eye of the semaphore; take succeeds take. At six-thirty they break for coffee and grape juice, which Ritscher and I collect from the café across the road; he tries his pidgin French on the woman behind the bar, whose ample breast reads "Denise." At 6:45, they essay a master tape. "I have the impression," says Straus, "that you think we don't have everything. But we do. You're being cautious; just play as if it were a performance, a concert." He tells me, sotto voce, "The break was too long." Take 31 is fine, however; Van Leeuwen agrees: "Yes, my dear."

"It's in the hand," says Straus. "The bag," Van Leeuwen corrects him. "The cat is in the bag."

At seven-thirty they begin the second movement. The first movement, with both repeats included, takes 14:14 of tape time, the third takes 8:15. They play the second movement through; it clocks in at 9:14. This will amount to thirty-two minutes of playing time and a dense single side of a record; twenty-eight minutes is optimal. Straus stops them at bar 7; "Your F is flat," he says. At bar 17, he stops them again. "It's not one hundred percent together." "Take it easy," Greenhouse suggests, "when you do that *subito*. You lose the whole effect of that *piano* after playing *forte*."

At 7:55, the red light goes on not because of performance error but because a truck has thundered past; onstage, the musicians are restive. The page turner, arrived at four, has not left her chair. I ask her if she's tired, if the time doesn't seem a bit long. She smiles up at me, revealing poor teeth. "It goes very quickly, I think." At bar 171, Cohen needs to correct a phrase; he performs it eight or nine times. Finally he has it. "And so on," he tells Giuranna, "into the night." "For safety's sake," says Straus at nine-fifteen, "let's try it one more time."

On Saturday night in La Chaux, the restaurants are full. The Philips personnel disperse, and the four musicians find an Italian restaurant. A violinist approaches. "I'll pay him," Cohen says, "to go away. You and your Gypsies," he sighs. We find a corner table and I ask them, once again, if the transition between live performance and recording is not a touch abrupt. Onstage and in concert they can do no wrong; in the studio, it seems, they can do nothing right. Pressler recollects how much records mattered to him when he was a student: the Schnabel Beethoven, he says, those 78s changed his life. "What offends me," says Giuranna, "is the substitution of the one for the other, the feeling that the record *is* the music. That's untrue." Volker's a perfectionist, they say; their earlier producers had been less precise. But he and Willem have been known to work ninety hours a week; in two full days, so far, they have recorded thirty-two minutes of music. They agree to reconvene on Sunday at eleven. "Wouldn't it be nice," Giuranna says, "to have a day off? Just once." "When did you take a day off?" Pressler asks. "When was a weekend a weekend?"

Across the street there is a coffee-bar with pinball machines, and a row of Pac-Mans; girls in designer jeans, their hands snugged into their rear pockets, sway to an inaudible beat. A boy with bright pink hair and a black leather jacket ambles past; he turns to enter the bar. There is a skull and crossbones on his jacket; the lettering reads "CHAOS." Giuranna urges a Sicilian wine upon us; Greenhouse orders squid.

La Chaux-de-Fonds sits twenty-three kilometers northwest of Neuchâtel and thirteen from the French border; it is a valley town. The main street hosts banks and watchmakers and retail and department stores; last year at this time, says Ritscher, the tree branches grew out of snow. "You must tunnel through the streets"—the piano tuner lifts his hands above his head—"*gewiss.*"

The hills surrounding town are studded with small chateaus. There are substantial stone and stucco houses on the steep pine slopes; on Sunday morning old people in furs take the air. Children are out in force also, on bicycles with skis for wheels or on homemade sleds; they shout at each other and cry for their parents to watch. Leashed dogs bark. It is a prosperous corner of Switzerland—solid to the point of stolid, and without display. A man sells chestnuts on the Avenue Léopold-Robert; a horsecart delivers milk.

Sunday morning the men rehearse the first movement of the G Minor Quartet. Downstairs, Straus and Van Leeuwen make preliminary notations on the E flat. They would like to return to Holland with at least an approximation of the selected takes; it takes Straus three times as long, he says, to work in Amsterdam. He prefers to sit in the same room and in the same position as when he first heard the performance; the ears take less adjusting. He has produced more than six hundred records for Philips (with such artists as Brendel, Grumiaux, Krips, and Nielsen); now he tapers off a bit and makes only—he smiles—twenty-two or three a year. He could have been a concert pianist, Van Leeuwen assures me; he has the hands.

The March 1980 issue of *Gramophone* (Volume 57, N. 682) contains a profile of Volker Straus. (Coincidentally, the cover of that issue features a Beaux Arts recording—the set of Haydn Trios—as record of the year for 1979. The magazine editors name it "far and away the winner . . . That the choice should now go to an issue in a relatively specialized category is a tribute to a monumental achievement, a landmark in the history of recorded chamber music.") Straus, who produced those records, addresses himself to a separate topic: that of the *Tonmeister*'s task. "Being a musician and a technician, I had to overcome the peculiarly nineteenth-century prejudice that says you can't be both. A musician was supposed to be a crazy, irrational man with long hair. This was his public image. On the other side there were the technicians—normal, rational men. If you go back to Bach's time there was no contradiction in terms between music, mathematics, and rational thinking. The old record companies, however, maintained this separatist attitude, but in 1950, when Philips started, the time was right to combine the two functions and train musicians to be engineers. Naturally, I think that is the best way."

Straus has kept track of the takes, and his reactions to each; in bars 121 to 127, for example, two of the five sounded acceptable. He marked the score accordingly, numbering the version that pleased him as well as the possible alternative; this morning, with Van Leeuwen playing them back, he listens to the indicated takes. If neither sounds adequate, he will compare them with the third-best version, and so on; if a note sounds less clear than he had hoped, he might indicate a selection from yet a fourth take—and splice in the correct note. When Van Leeuwen does not need to hunt and play a passage, he peruses a book on Alfred Brendel; they will meet with Brendel in London the following week. Robert Ritscher enters. "*Hast gut geschlafen?*" he asks. Straus waves him away from the speakers and the "sound line" to his right; Ritscher sits.

Onstage the musicians confer. "Do you think it would be possible," Giuranna asks, "to change a little bit the color? I think before B it should have a little smoother character than the figure in the beginning." "Just now," says Cohen, "I find the triplets a little breezy. Shall we do it once slowly"—he sings the phrase—"letting me exaggerate to see if I am too far?"

Again they play and pause. "My E doesn't come together—Menahem, are you going to do both lines *pianissimo*?" "Yes," Pressler answers. "Let's start from E. I don't think the two *sforzandi* are equal." "You prefer the second one more?" "No. Less." "We have to decide on the bowing," Cohen says. "I'll do anything you want. What I find difficult is that we're not together on the second D; Menahem, you're separating between the D and the G; the note should be extremely well placed." "It's embellishment," Giuranna says. "It's a bit sentimental, that phrase." "It wasn't my intention to make it sentimental at all—more a statement of the theme, a pronunciation of each note." "Still," Greenhouse interjects, "it sounds sentimental to me. . . ."

The strings agree. "Eight bars before the G, I think we make a useless accent on the downbeat. This scale does not reach a dissonance as does the next bar—otherwise, we'll get an accent every bar. Let's try to make a tremendous line to the *forte*, from the viola solo—why not?"

Giuranna and Cohen spend some minutes attempting different bowings on a unison passage. "I have the feeling," says Cohen, "that the harmony change should push us. But we pushed the harmony change." "This is one of the masterworks," Giuranna says, "because it goes already a little against the idea of the always smiling Mozart." Pressler concurs. "The only thing that matches it is the two-viola quintet." Giuranna is courtly, urbane. Cohen tapes a *Playboy* centerfold to the inside of his score, hoping to distract him; Giuranna does not falter but swears his vibrato improves. "For A," he says, "I promise you the best vibrato I have. But you have to give me A first." "For your best vibrato," says Pressler, hitting the key twice, "you can have two As."

We lunch at the Hôtel Moreau. Again there are good humor and bad jokes, a sense of forward motion with the work. They have completed the E flat ahead of schedule, in less than half the time allotted for both quartets. By my count they have been playing together—exclusive of individual practice time—for twenty-three hours. Lunch consists of ham and endives baked in béchamel sauce; the waitress is flustered, apologetic. "It's Sunday," she says, "and nobody works. So nobody has any time." We tell her not to worry, and she says, "Musicians. I tell everyone they're the patient customers. I Musici, they come here." Giuranna looks surprised. "And that little man," she continues, "the nice one, what's his name. Claudio."

"Abaddo?" Cohen asks.

"Arrau," says Pressler.

"Cardinale," I offer. "Claudio Cardinale."

"*Si,*" she says. "That's it. Claudio Cardinale"—and proceeds to take our orders for dessert.

At four they commence to record. The page turner confesses she went dancing and slept until two in the afternoon; she drank black coffee for lunch. There is the by-now familiar litany from Straus: "Bar 86 is too loud; bar 165, violin and cello are too loud; 191, the C of the viola could be clearer." Sometimes he's diplomatic ("Yes, sorry, I think that in bar 134 if you don't make too much of an accent on the B flat, it will be better"), sometimes blunt ("In 122 the high D was flat"), sometimes all-embracing ("Everybody makes a crescendo from 128, and that's a problem still"). At six-thirty the musicians request coffee, and he says, "Yes. A good idea." He turns to me and confides, "They're paying a bit for yesterday, for having done two movements. It will be fantastic when it's finished, but today they're overdoing it. Forcing. But you know, in G minor—it's the same with the G Minor Symphony—there's no consolation. No moment in which Mozart allows you to say, *Voilà,* everything's fine. It's just over."

I ask for his assessment of the Trio as ensemble, his sense of how they work. "Fantastic," he says readily. "And they're so different, so absolutely different, what they bring. Bernie's the rock. The fundamental." Straus makes a fist. "He has a metronome in his head, he's absolutely exact. And Izzy is the artist, the philosopher, a little bit of Gypsy in him, too. And Menahem"—he punches the air—"is, how would you call it, energy? The driving force."

At seven-thirty Greenhouse says, "It's starting to sound like something now; we're getting warm." Take 9 sounds plausible; take 16, at eight-fifteen, has a flaw in bar 196. They play the coda repeatedly. By nine-thirty (and take

26), Straus presses the green-light button several times. "That's it," he says over the phone. "The cat's in the hand." "Yes, my dear," says Van Leeuwen, "in the bag."

Monday and Tuesday follow the same pattern—the second movement recorded on Monday afternoon and the third on Tuesday. They require slightly less rehearsal time by now and spend more time in the control room, listening to tapes. On their previous visit to La Chaux, they recorded the Beethoven Septet (in its transcription for piano trio); Straus invites their reaction to his master tape. Pressler is uneasy at the pace of the opening measures; Straus assures him it can be fixed. Photographers from Philips and the local newspapers appear. They discuss the next recording dates, and the literature: Schubert most probably, and Chausson and Ravel. Giuranna will be at the Marlboro Music Festival in July; they invite him to join them for a "Mostly Mozart" performance in New York. Giuranna accepts; they will offer both quartets and let the presentor decide. Greenhouse produces a bottle of whiskey for the last listening session, and Ritscher swallows enthusiastically; his young wife won't forgive him, he says, when he returns with this stomach.

A friend of Greenhouse, living in Geneva, brings his son to the Hôtel Moreau for an impromptu cello lesson; the boy is rapt. Attention shifts to the forthcoming tour, and travel arrangements. The musicians leave on Wednesday—the Trio for Paris, Giuranna for Rome. Straus and Van Leeuwen remain till Thursday night. Straus is an avid amateur sailor, as is Greenhouse; they discuss their respective boats. When he gets the chance, says Straus, he will recondition his brightwork and the wood; he has three sons who help. The hotel manager bids the Trio a voluble farewell. They will return for a concert at Théâtre Musica on January 21, and for the Schubert recording in May. A Spanish chambermaid pushes the cart full of luggage three streets to the station. She likes this country, she tells me, the mountains, the climate; it is a good place to work. The weather has held cold and clear.

Chapter Six

Menahem Pressler was born Max Menahem Pressler in Magdeburg, Germany, on December 16, 1923. He emigrated with his family to Palestine, where his serious study of music began; he now spends as much time as possible in Israel. Home, however, is Bloomington, Indiana—where he maintains a full-time teaching load at Indiana University's School of Music. He and his wife, Sarah, have two children: a son, Ami, a laboratory technician, and a daughter, Edna, a student at Smith College.

Pressler first journeyed to America after World War II, speaking next to no English and as a contestant in the Debussy Competition. He won first prize. He made his resulting debut with Eugene Ormandy and the Philadelphia Orchestra; he has appeared as soloist with, among others, the New York Philharmonic, the Cleveland Symphony, the National Symphony, and the Royal Philharmonic Orchestra of London.

Public men repeat themselves in their frequent interviews; if you get something right, why vary it for the next set of ears? Pressler was particularly happy with an article by Jeffrey Wagner in *Clavier*, May/June, 1982. He commended it to me as something worth repeating; I have done so below. The footnotes indicate those paragraphs of the piece I here reprint.

This interview took place in bits and snatches—in hotel rooms, at restaurants, on trains. That feels characteristic of Pressler, a man in seeming-perpetual motion. Most often we met late at night: the pianist in his cardigan, puffing a cigar. He hunts, he says, for the twenty-fifth hour in every day, the extra day each month; his schedule is impossible, he says, what with the teaching load, the master classes in Kansas; "Don't ask what I'm doing this year." . . . Diminutive, cherubic, he speaks with a strong accent and punctuates language with gesture; the energy of his public performance remains intact offstage. My questions are indicated by the abbreviation "Int.," his answers by his initials "M.P."

Int.: Let's begin with first things first—your early memories of music, your discovery of a vocation and first influence.

M.P.: My earliest memories of course go back to Germany—where I actually started to study the violin for a little while. But my brother started the piano, and I always listened to him and was attracted by it; after a while I had to make a decision, so I studied the piano. My parents were Zionists, and our visa arrived at the last minute; we traveled from Trieste to Haifa just when Italy had declared war. And so it was truly by luck that we arrived. I remember I was already playing on that ship, playing for the captain's table maybe, and I took lessons while we waited in Trieste. My first serious teacher was in Palestine, a man by the name of Eliahu Rudiakow. He had come from Russia, and had studied in Germany with Max Pauer; he was a fine person and very warm, sympathetic to the trauma of emigration and the adjustments I had had to make.

Then I studied with Leo Kestenberg, a pupil of Busoni's. He had been a member of the German musical and intellectual circles, an official in the Ministry for Fine Arts. He was not as fine a pianist as

Rudiakow, but he had great erudition in the literature; he influenced me to "read between the lines."

I remember how we studied the *Diabelli* Variations of Beethoven, for example. Of course, this is one of the great masterpieces, and also a kind of ABC for Beethoven's music. I believe it was Bülow who was supposed to have said that if we lost everything of Beethoven, we could reconstruct it from the *Diabelli*. Now, this is surely an exaggeration, but it shows how marvelous and comprehensive the work is, doesn't it?—a kind of key. I also remember studying with Kestenberg the three Opus 31 of Beethoven. You know, I found the three of them together a marvelous kaleidoscope: with the first in G major, clear as a brook; the second in D minor, full of complexes and passions, *fermatas*, and drama (even the key, D minor, is not very typical for Beethoven); and the E-flat Sonata, which is virtuosic in character. Kestenberg showed me the Beethoven who could be esoteric and philosophical in one moment, and vulgar—or, as the Germans say, *grob*—in the next. I think this is what brings Beethoven so close to us, isn't it, that he can be so human as well as heavenly and refined.[1]

Int.: During the war in Palestine, there could not have been much "live" performing. You've spoken of hearing Schnabel on 78s; was the gramophone your concert hall?

M.P.: Yes; at that time, the country was closed. I was deeply impressed when I heard the second Brahms Concerto played by someone who has disappeared—at least I've never heard his name again. It was an Englishman in an English Army uniform—and though I may be mistaken as to his name, the second Brahms left an indelible impression. Then a French pianist played in Israel—Paul Loyonnet, a man who never again made a great reputation. But he needed someone to accompany him on second piano with the orchestra—and someone recommended me. So I did it and he liked it. Then he asked me what I was going to do, and I had read in the paper about a competition in San Francisco—the Debussy Prize. I told him about Debussy, that I would enter the competition, and I played some Debussy for him. He told me certain things about it, gave me certain insights. And because he came from the French tradition, he opened some doors for me; I walked through them on my own after that, but I would credit him for having shown me that there is a door to walk through. My daughter believes in luck, that a Sagittarius has this kind of luck.

So I got a ticket and flew from Tel Aviv to Cairo, then to Geneva, Paris, and, finally, New York. I had had another bit of luck; I had been introduced in Israel to an American impresario by the name of Rabinoff who said—this complete stranger—when you arrive in America, before you come, send me a telegram, I'll pick you up at the airport. My plane was delayed in Cairo, and we arrived in New York at three-thirty in the morning, and there was a note from him, saying, "Don't worry. I'm outside waiting for you." He found me a room at a hotel and he brought me down to the Steinway basement—amazing—and a tuner came along, and Rabinoff said, "Let the boy try out some pianos." So I played a little, and the tuner said, "Don't play on this piano. Try that one; that is what Schnabel always uses." Then I tried Beethoven, and he said, "This is what Casadesus uses." I played some Debussy, and he said, "Just a minute," and walked upstairs and brought down Mr. Steinway. And I played for Mr. Steinway. He said, "What are you doing here?" and I told him I was getting ready for the competition and he said, "Fine. You may need a place to practice. You can have this basement."

Then someone told me, "Don't go to the competition. It's fixed anyway in advance." But I had promised so many people in Israel that I would go no matter what. I felt I had to go to the competition. And I went and won first prize. Then Rabinoff arranged for me to have an audition for Arthur Judson, the president of Columbia Artists. He was the South Pole of management; there was Hurok at the North Pole and Judson at the South. I played for him; he took me as an artist, and I am still with them today.

Int.: It doesn't sound entirely like luck.

M.P.: No, not entirely. But unless you're guided, all these things come with much greater difficulty. And Judson arranged for me to have an audition with Ormandy, who engaged me to make my debut with the Philadelphia Orchestra in Carnegie Hall. All this was fabulous, a great deal of luck at the start. Then I also spent a summer with Egon Petri at Mills College in Oakland. This was after I had made my debut—a very intensive summer. His first question—he could be rather blunt, actually—was to ask why I wanted to study with him. He thought I seemed "finished." He was a fine man and teacher, and his approach was very different from mine. For him, everything was filtered through the brain, and only then came the heart. The passions were controlled, thought about. On the other hand I was, and still am, very emotional; I make a lot of motions at the keyboard. I have to laugh when I think of how he once asked me, "Tell me, does the keyboard smell good to you; why is your nose down so close to it?" So, he would make these remarks, and it was good for me. Even when I found I had to disagree with him, in the disagreement I found my own answers.[2]

Int.: You've described a series of very different teachers, a separate set of pedagogical approaches. Could you pinpoint what you responded to—which ones were successful, which failed—and also perhaps what you've extracted from those strategies now that the roles are reversed?

M.P.: I am always telling my students to be like a bee, to take ideas from wherever they can be taken, and then make their own honey from them. Today I'm a conglomeration of all those things that happened in my life and that somehow made an impression on me—the scents and distillations from which I made my honey. Maybe something very important passed by me, but, on the other hand, something that to someone else may have seemed unimportant would create within me a sense of excitement. You can't be satisfied with an answer from someone else, no matter how great his knowledge or experience. You must use that experience to stand on his shoulders, in order to see for yourself, to use your own eyes, your own ears, your own heart, your own mind. I studied with a person whom I thought a fabulous musician—Edvard Steuermann. This was a very important association for me. I was touring regularly by then, but even so he influenced me in many ways. Many of my insights into the Schumann *Fantasia* began then, for example.

The most important dimension in my musical education came through the Beaux Arts Trio. I know it may seem strange at first, because we are now talking about musicians who are not pianists; but you see, they are musicians from the pure point of view. We talk about music, as it sounds to us, as it speaks to us. Playing chamber music has added so many more aspects to my way of hearing and playing music. For example, in chamber music you do not sectionalize as much, by virtue of the fact that you usually give the theme to another musician. You do not take a rest the way a young soloist usually does: you know, they play one beautiful phrase, and then they sit and wait for the next one to come around. It often lacks the sense of continuity that chamber music demands. You become much more conscious of balance with the other instruments and with yourself, between one hand and the other, between two different voices in the piano part.

You know, as a young man, I was told, "Play chamber music. It's good for you." But it was always in such a way that it sounded like taking medicine. We all know how wonderful it is to sight-read chamber music for the fun of it, with friends and colleagues, and there is nothing wrong with that; but there the attitude is casual: "Oh, you want it this way? Fine. You want it that way? That's fine too. A little slower? Wonderful." But chamber music is serious business, too. For us, it's blood, sweat, and tears; you really work; you really do it to achieve something. You see, in chamber music, as in your solo playing, the idea is to create a face which the listeners recognize. A face in which you are you, and not just one of many. When you hear the masters, they are distinctive, you recognize them easily. You may like what they do, or you may not like it, but you will always recognize what they are doing.[3]

Int.: As a teacher of writing, I have a limited sense of possibility. I think that the best writing teacher has never "created" a writer where there wasn't a student who could become one. And perhaps, though this is difficult to prove, the worst writing teacher has never destroyed a truly substantial talent.

M.P.: It's the people on the fence. Either you can make something out of them or not. A teacher can play a very big role with those marginal cases; I do feel that I help. I help, I would say, on a number of levels. First, there's the professional, the knowledge of music—and I can instill at least that which has been taught to me. Then I like them to feel the love, that a life in music is a beautiful life, and this in spite of success or not. The student can feel they live a life that's positive; they don't feel "I am not worth it; oh, I have lost out." Sure, with success you enjoy many more things—but there is already something when you hear yourself play in private, when you repeat those works of a Mozart or a Beethoven: everyone who has added something to the richness of our emotional repertoire. And that, I think, is important; a teacher can be of help there.

Int.: What do you look for in a student; how do you select those with whom you choose to work?

M.P.: I always take on some students I realize will not be the best players but might make good teachers. I remember one student who was very bad, really very poor, but she played for me the Brahms A Minor Intermezzo from his Opus 116, and I've never heard that piece played so well. I have never loved that piece more than during the moments she played it for me. Teaching can be instructive to the teacher. I like the saying which comes, I believe, from the Talmud: "I learned a great deal from my teachers, I learned even more from myself, and I learned most of all from my students." For me, teaching is absolutely as fulfilling as performance. I think the proof is that I could fill my schedule with concerts at this point, but I want very much to teach, to share experiences in this way, to have a meeting of minds, an opening of minds. I suppose it is somewhat parental in a way, the older teacher and the younger student relationship, but what is really marvelous is that your students usually want to hear what you have to say.[4] Real children don't always want to hear their parents; sometimes, with your own children, it is not what you have and what you are capable of giving that they need. There is still that love, of course, and that blood relationship—but your life takes on a double meaning for your students, because it enriches theirs. I got a present just now of lilies; on the first day they looked really like nothing; on the second day they opened up, and I added water, and it was a joy to see. . . .

Int.: Technical proficiency is important to you, clearly. And I have heard you speak of "character" in students; could you amplify on that?

M.P.: First of all I look for coordination, to see that the hands are good. I look for intelligence, so that I will know that they can understand what I have to say, and I look for that unspecific thing called character. You can't be anything with only wonderful fingers or a great memory. You will only be a playing machine that doesn't amount to much. No, there must be that ability to go through thick and thin as a musician as well as a person. You need a good sense of inner discipline, a guiding force, to succeed. That's what I would like to find in a student. I might even say that if I see this quality, I will take them on even though they may have started late or may not be accomplished players. I look for the kind of student who will learn enough about music so that he or she may in turn become a teacher. You see, there is great repertoire to be played by people who do not have those fast and agile fingers, who maybe will never play the twenty-seven etudes of Chopin . . . I always enjoy a beautiful phrase more than fast octaves, although the great octave player can be very exciting, too. It can be like going to the circus; I love it for what it's worth, but it's not worth a very great deal, really.

Int.: Once you select a student, what are your teaching methods—do you have a particular program or approach that's subject to generalization? Or is it in every instance a specific response to the stimulus provided?

M.P.: Well, you must build a relationship first. You have to build a mutual vocabulary. You see, we must learn to understand one another so that when I say "relax," they know exactly what I mean by that. Most students, I find, have not been taught well technically, and normally we have to work on this.

So we usually begin with exercises, abstract exercises. People ask, "Why not use difficult spots in real pieces to practice technique?" This is all right, but when you have to concentrate and learn to use your muscles, I think it is best to concentrate completely on the physical aspect of playing the instrument, and to photograph, so to speak, what you are doing when you learn to do it right.

Then, as a first piece, we choose a work that is perhaps not the most difficult, but one which will apply those techniques we have learned. Chopin etudes are ideal at that point. They make one study how to use the arm, how to move the fingers, the wrist, and so forth, and at the same time they demand that you become conscious of sonority, of the music. Because they are not too long, this helps the concentration. The next piece will be larger, often a Beethoven sonata or a Schumann work. I adore Schumann. His riches are so deep and so marvelous that at this point I use him to prick the soul and make the imagination soar.

Int.: How do you diagnose what a student needs?

M.P.: I find both what they do well and also what they don't. I always let them do what they do best. I think, however, they should also develop what they are not good at, even if only to help them in what they are already good at.

A problem that often comes up is when a student wants to play a piece that I don't feel they can handle yet. However, I usually encourage them to take it because very often, if they desire it so much, working on it will help them advance a step. Often it proves to be not as difficult for them as I had thought. The effort, the love, the desire they spend on it will help them get a few steps up the ladder. I rarely say simply, "That's too difficult for you, and we can't do it." It is such a dried-out notion, that one must play this piece only at a certain time and only after having studied other specified repertoire. If carried to the extreme, as in some European conservatories, it's quite fatal to teach that way. We must do anything to help a person find his maximum. How few do find it. I want them to be motivated and to continue after their degree, after getting a job, and so forth. I want them to keep their desire no matter where they end up, because that place where they are is the musical center for them. If you continue to live that way, you will make yourself happy, and you will make others around you happy. You will not feel that you are just a poor pianist who makes a poor salary, but that you are a rich man.

Int.: How do you view competitions and how do you advise your students who want to enter them?

M.P.: I have been fortunate to have my students do well in them, and I do encourage it. It's a necessity, really, almost a way of life for the young performer. But very few pianists are good at competitions. These are unusual circumstances, and few do their best under them. Because there are many members of a jury, all too often, they simply choose the one who offends the least, the one they can agree on. It's terrible for the ones who are second and third or, even worse, for a real talent who does not advance past the first round; that happens, too. It's unavoidable under the circumstances.

So I try to help my students prepare psychologically to be winners and losers; both are difficult, incidentally. It is difficult for the student who loses to still stand up and know that he is going in the right way, toward goals that are important, much more important than a competition. Ultimately it is not the prize or the reviews that matter very much but the way in which you see yourself growing in relation to music.[5]

Int.: Let's shift the focus here a little and speak of your own preparations, your way of remaining a student. You practice, for instance, continually. . . .

M.P.: I love to practice. There are people who don't like to because it's hard work—but at home I have dinner and have two hours' sleep, then I ask my wife to wake me, and begin. I wish I could practice more, but there's only a limited time available—so therefore I must practice what I need. In music you have the athletics—that means the hands have to be in order—and you have the understanding of the piece—therefore, you practice that work—and then you have the peak of the pyramid, which is the artistic expression. This doesn't come by chance; it is based on your professionalism, your musical understanding, your ability at a given moment to read between the lines. You must find the key.

Int.: Can you put that process into words, that system of discovery?

M.P.: The words are prosaic: you practice. Most people know that they have to practice their hands; very few people know that they have to practice their souls. You believe that the inspiration of the moment will carry you—and, true, very often it does. But that is when the wind is at your back, and you sail very easily; you must learn to sail when the wind is in your face.

Int.: When you prepare a performance, do you study other interpretations or avoid them? How much research do you do?

M.P.: As a young boy, I would sometimes do that sort of research; it truly doesn't mean much. It's like learning something phonetically; you speak in a strange language phonetically; you pronounce the words correctly but not with the feel of the whole. The true meaning you can derive only from work with the work; I must have the work talk to me. So you play and study and teach a work, and naturally you learn a language and the vocabulary of a particular composer. What I do find now—after I've lived with Mozart, Schumann, Brahms, and so on—is that the more I read, the more refinements, nuances, shadings, meanings I discover; after all, we are a composite of emotions triggered by certain things. Now you must learn what triggers you, what brings you to express yourself; you must bring it out in such a way that what is meaningful for you becomes meaningful for the listener.

Int.: Could you identify some of those triggers—some of those touchstones and the process of transference?

M.P.: First of all I respond to a refinement that I may find in a phrase. I look for it, knowing by now the picture; now I look for a certain light, a certain shading for myself that renews this piece. Now, where is that? I don't always know in advance. Let me say that what is so beautiful about this process is that it changes; this makes it possible for me to go out and play a certain piece over and over. I feel that in order to play Schubert you have to *be* a Schubert, to play Beethoven you have to *be* a Beethoven. And for that I have to be a worker in the coal mines, I must dig deep; the road is wonderful, the digging is wonderful; that desire to *be* Schubert is one of the great things. And it's a source of energy, it reproduces itself. It seems to be like that drop of water that re-creates its own energy. I have disregarded age a little bit; I feel blessed.

Int.: Is there a particular literature, a particular series of composers for whom you feel the greatest affinity—and do such preferences change?

M.P.: It's very hard to say. There was a time, in the beginning—when I won the Debussy Prize—when the Impressionists attracted me. I found them rich and still do. Then Chopin grew very meaningful to me; now I feel more and more strongly about Beethoven, his coarseness and depth and virtuosity, and Schubert, that endless song. . . . If I were to make my ideal program, it would consist of Mozart, Beethoven, Schubert, Schumann, Brahms. There are other very great composers, of course. You don't hear me mention Bach; I love him, but to me he does not fill the spaces of my soul. This can change, of course; I mean there was a time in my life when Liszt played a great role, but I don't feel that way anymore; I find his rhetoric pompous, a little. I still love certain works that he has written, but not *him* as much as I used to. Still, we should be jealous of ourselves, what we have at our disposal. . . .

Int.: I've been struck in rehearsal by how often you—or other members of the Trio—have said in effect, "I find this mannered, I find it exaggerated, I find this too dramatic." You seem to suggest that the performer should not "get between" the composer and his work, that restraint is the appropriate posture. And is this also an attitude subject to change over time; did you feel that way, for instance, when performing Liszt?

M.P.: When you play a Mozart whose music comes to you direct and pure, you react spontaneously. Certain moments in him are very dramatic and you react dramatically; certain moments are very refined and you act, in that moment, refined. But when you put it together as a piece of art, a performance, you must *sieve*, you must act as if it's a soup. And you take all the roughage away. Because that which is between you and the composer is all right, but between you and the composer and the performance of the piece in front of an audience, it's wrong. You see, you have to distill, you must distill, and then it's pure and clear and clean again. Now, in order to distill you must exaggerate, you must go through those moments, that response; you must try to find the borders of the style. There are different borders, and they are defined by taste—and you must acquire taste, to learn it over time.

Int.: What of a composer whose work changed radically: Beethoven. Should the early Sonatas be played first, and then the late?

M.P.: Yes, some of them. Few of us have time to learn all the early Sonatas. You should progress in this way, of course, from early to late. If you were to start right off with the late ones, it would be like reading a book in a foreign language in such a way that you had to look up every word with a dictionary in one hand and the book in the other. You must know the ABCs first.

Then, in the later work, his soul became rarefied. These works seem to express philosophical concepts besides the sound, besides the technique of their composition. I love these late works for what they mean to me not only as a musician, but also as a man. I love to play them for what I know they can do to others, and I love to teach them because of what they can open up in a student. Younger artists may not have as great a capacity for seeing and understanding these works, but this is what we strive for. This is what these works demand: to see ever more clearly, more deeply, without ever stopping, without ever being really satisfied. I am always finding so much more in these works—Opus 110, for instance. I can't drink in enough of it. It is so fulfilling, so satisfying to hear the fugue, so organically complete. Some say the piece is rather autobiographical: The first movement is Beethoven the idealist, the second one Beethoven the hedonist, the third is Beethoven full of grief, of despair, of regret, the Beethoven who sings the *klagendes Gesang* ("plaintive song"). And the fugue—the fugue is so naturally a fulfillment of all of this, as if it had grown organically. So many special moments: the G-major chords—one can spend hours building them, hearing them, feeling them.[6]

Int.: This reduction of personality of which you speak—this increase in reportage with reference to the original text—is there a point at which that yields diminishing returns?

M.P.: Of course, one does never know what the composer had in mind. I firmly believe that after it's been written down, it becomes your property if you make it so. I mean, most performers become a Xerox machine. They can give you a wonderful clean copy back, which gets thinner and thinner as time goes on and the ink runs out. Now there was a time—before my time—when a performer such as Kreisler or Rachmaninoff, for instance, would change all the dynamic markings and make the piece in his image. Now you've got to be godlike to make it in your image. On the other hand, when you have a great familiarity with this matter and it becomes a part of you, you hear it inside of you continually. And so I take certain liberties; I am convinced of them, I feel them at this point. When one gets older, one loses certain things. Such as daring—one becomes more careful, more concerned. But you gain something. There is an insight which comes with age, experience, the knowledge of what the end is like. When you are young, you never know what the end of the piece is like; there is no such thing as continual gain; you gain and you lose.

Int.: Do you ever wish to stay home and plant a garden? What is the potential loss in a situation so manifestly full of gain as is your present career?

M.P.: I haven't yet found the need to cultivate a garden. Yes, I would have wanted, from time to time, more of a chance to study and reflect; I haven't even heard the latest records we made, for instance. Right now I'm like a person who takes all the pictures on a trip and doesn't have time to look at them. He hopes he will be given the time when he can put up his feet and look at those pictures and enjoy them—but right now I enjoy the taking, the doing. Yes, I am impassioned with it, I am thirsty, I am still as hungry with it as I remember having been when young.

Int.: We have now touched on two of your careers—those of teacher and of soloist. You have made your reputation, however, principally as a chamber musician. Do you feel that the nature of solo performance is essentially at odds with that of the chamber musician, or are they two sides of the same coin?

M.P.: I think, yes, it's two sides of the same coin. You do what you are permitted to do. For a pianist, it's different than for many of the string players. I started accidentally to play chamber music; by nature I fitted, I was good at it. I became better at it. I developed facilities that are very important in order to do it—a certain acquisition of empathy, a subordination of the ego. Many used to feel, if you can't play solo you play chamber music, but that's not the case at all. I came into chamber music with two wonderful colleagues; I have always found that a great joy. I don't want to minimize the difficulties, but these things pass—and that which you achieve together is lasting.

Int.: This lastingness is one of the hallmarks of the Trio. I can think of a string quartet or two—the Amadeus, the Juilliard (though in the latter instance, there's been much change in personnel)—who have been in existence longer than the Trio. But you have established a standard of longevity with this literature.

M.P.: More than that; we have established the piano trio. When we started, there was no such thing. There was the literature, of course, the repertoire—but everyone assumed that a form could not be achieved. Either it's a poor man's piano concerto—two strings and half a piano—or it's one person accompanying two soloists; that was the common assumption. We did it, however; we achieved a sense of balance that is to this day unequaled. It was always a major literature, of course. But three splendid fellows would get together to play Schubert. . . . There are great examples, and I love every minute of it, the chance to listen to Cortot, Thibaud, Casals. Or Rubinstein, Piatigorsky, and Heifetz. Just to hear them tune would have been sufficient; it's gorgeous—but truly a trio it isn't. Everyone follows his own flight of fancy. There is no real work with one outline—so that when we hear them we love what Casals has to say. We do the same with Cortot and Thibaud—but we love Schubert the less. He does not seem central. You take three eggs, even if they are elephant eggs, and out must come cake. You put something in and what comes out must be greater than the sum of the parts—a direction in which you move together, an interpretation that is refined, established. With some of the great virtuosi—I don't want here to mention names, and I'm not thinking of those I mentioned above—the greater the work, the less well it sounds; the lesser the work, the more fantastic it sounds. That is not our way.

Int.: Would you venture a description of the Trio's "parts" —what each of you in particular contributed to the whole?

M.P.: Daniel Guilet, with his tremendous experience, had a sense of inspiration. This may not have come across as strongly to the audience as it did to us. And he had an insight—into the works of Beethoven and, naturally, the French composers—a strong sense of holding the work at the fore, of keeping one's emotions in check for the sake of the piece. Not to be lenient with the feelings—he would insist on that. This was very strong in Guilet, and I learned from him in that respect more than I'd learned from my teachers. I would hear it as an assertion, but not as a felt truth: the way you hear milk is good for you, motherhood is holy, the fatherland should be defended, and so forth. But very often you hear—more, perhaps, with soloists—a strong reaction to a certain passage, and this comes at the expense of something else, a unity.

Bernie's beauty of sonority is inspiring. He has one of the most gorgeous sounds I know; I've played with him now for twenty-seven years, and I'm still in love with the way he expresses himself on the cello, his sonority, his sensitivity to a phrase. This is something to which I also aspire and brought into the playing—the so-called piano sonority.

Int.: Has the face of the Beaux Arts Trio altered greatly over time—and with particular reference to the change of violinists?

M.P.: It has certainly changed. When Izzy came in, with his particular talent—he had devoted himself to chamber music so intensely—he entered the group and followed the outlines already there. But then, of course, while he adjusted to us, we also had to adjust to his personality, his intentions. The approach altered. We are to a certain extent more literary; it's in part a tenor of the times. To some extent Izzy persuaded us of this; we used to be much less literal in terms of the musical markings.

What has not changed in myself—and, I'm sure, in Bernie—is that sense of looking for the unique experience in the piece. And the great moment cannot be reached through the brain. The brain takes you only so far; it is something in your soul, in your inner makeup, in your inner ear, and that's what you ask for—that time should stand still. That's what I remember from great performances that have stayed with me to this day; it's not the complete performance. I remember those moments. . . . It's like when you go to Bocuse and he is in form; he can't cook that way every day. So something very special happens on the rare inspired evening—whether you attend it to listen or perform.

What is very curious in a group like the Beaux Arts is that we have a dynamic of our own—there's a dynamism separate from each of us alone. If you work against it, it just won't go. So we will try it this way, then that way—but it comes down to a dynamic of its own. In his autobiography, Carl Flesch tells a story of how Schnabel insisted that their trio—Schnabel, Becker, and Flesch—do something one way. They fought and fought, but Schnabel was irrepressible. So, at the next rehearsal when they played it that way, Schnabel got very upset and wondered how anyone could ever play it this way. They replied that it had been his idea, to which he answered that he had changed and grown. Sometimes you are absolutely convinced of something, even though you may later change your opinions or your convictions. This has something to do with inspiration, I think, which is spontaneous. That is ten percent of any performance.

Sometimes it is as though you press a certain button and all of a sudden it illuminates, clarifies, connects, beautifies. The sound takes on a sheen that you always try for but do not always get. Then all of a sudden you have it. You may see something in a phrase of Schubert, maybe, that you have played hundreds of times and suddenly it seems so obvious, so clear, so deep, so warm.

So you try to press the button of inspiration. It is unpredictable, though. This is why we performers are always a little worried. You worry because you know that you may play well, but that if you are not inspired, it will not take on that special dimension, like flying. How seldom, how very seldom, that happens.[7]

Int.: The convention still pertains that the soloist should learn the music by heart, whereas the chamber musician need not. Do you find this a useful distinction?

M.P.: I don't think he really must. I remember one of the most beautiful evenings, a Beethoven evening given by Dame Myra Hess in Indianapolis; she had someone sitting there with the music, although she didn't look at it once. Strangely enough, as you get older it becomes a worry, and with the pieces you learn later on. I can remember the early pieces all right, but memory fails. Toscanini started it because he couldn't see well, and he had that phenomenal memory; after that it became *à la mode.* Yet today a great conductor, a man like Solti, uses the score. Music is an aural experience mainly—you get it through your ears. It's true that when you watch a performer, you get influenced either by his histrionics or his lack of histrionics; you get influenced by energy—but what is most important is what we hear.

I've also found that so many things which seemed important when young are not necessary; you believe that success will come because you do this, that and the other, but it isn't like that—it comes to meet you halfway. One of the ways that I measure success is that people are willing to pay you; after all, they will fly you to Monte Carlo for a concert. . . . I mean, this is very surprising. Three old gentlemen come out onstage, with their potbellies and no hair, and sit down to make music and get paid!

Int.: You often refer to tradition, to a legacy that has been left or that you hope to leave. This sense of the ensemble so crucial to chamber music making—does it extend to your audience, your students, your somewhat more distant colleagues as well?

M.P.: What we would like to leave is this belief in balance—that players go into chamber music because they so choose, not because they can't do anything else. I would also like to say that life in a trio is a very beautiful one. If one can keep the respect and the friendship of his colleagues—because that is not easy, the day-after-day association, the release of aggressions—it is wonderful to share a success, as well as it is comforting and strengthening to share a defeat. Because both are in your way, both come your way, and all of this is made more bearable by company. You know, people marry for some of the same reasons; sex is not the only thing. We used to say that we've been married for twenty-seven years, only without the advantages; all the disadvantages we've got. But we have this one great advantage—companionship in music making that interests us alike.

I want to be an honest musician. At least, I would like to repeat the score as if I see it through the original eyes of the composer. But then I look for that part of me that responds to inspiration—and that is what I would like to give someone because I know what it means to me. I hope to speak to fifty-one percent of the audience, which is already a triumphant proportion. I know how to prepare myself physically, how to get my head in order, and I am prepared to listen with, so to speak, the third ear; when the moment comes I will try to grasp it. It is something to live for, something to strive for, something that enriches you. And that search drives me, the hunt for it; there is my motor.

I come home from teaching sometimes and listen to a recording or the radio, and my wife says, "What? You're teaching all day, or practicing, or away on tour, and you still want more music when you come home?" I say that I must have it, I cannot get enough of it. It sustains me.

1. "Menahem Pressler, Multifaceted Musician," *Clavier*, May/June 1982, p. 15.
2. Ibid., pp. 15–16.
3. Ibid., p. 16.
4. Ibid.
5. Ibid., pp. 17–18.
6. Ibid., p. 18.
7. Ibid.

Chapter Seven

The career of the successful touring artist is the stuff of dreams. Night after night when the stage lights come up, they do so to the music of applause. Bejeweled ladies faint or fling themselves beneath the wheels of carriages. The beautiful ones leave their room keys. Audiences scramble to greet the virtuoso; they bear caviar and cases of Champagne. Boats and trains and planes and limousines are waiting; a manager hovers helpfully at the railroad station and in the concert-hall wings. The hotels are deluxe. There are interviews, receptions, the wide world a stage and the player triumphal upon it. . . .

Some of this is true. Yet that insubstantial pageant is such stuff as dreams are made on; look at it more closely and it will dissolve. A performer logs as many miles as a pilot every month, but work begins after the ride. He cannot cancel because of bad weather or distance; he may have a headache, a backache, a stomachache; he may not see his wife or children on their birthdays or on holidays; he must smile at importunate strangers who say, "Remember me?" He does not get any younger, any thinner; his sightseeing consists of the inside of greenrooms and single beds in cities far from home.

Between these twinned polarities, a season of touring extends. The Beaux Arts Trio play, on average, 130 concerts per year. Since Pressler lives in Bloomington, the three can never meet in Manhattan and retire after the concert; at least one of them is always on the road. A representative season will include three trips to Europe, three in North America, and one to South America, Australia, or the Far East. There are variations on this theme, of course, and sometimes things get "easy"; they may remain three days in town—for a festival or master class, or because of a free date. Those free dates are, however, the exception not the rule; a twenty-one-day tour includes eighteen concerts at least. And the pattern of concert-hall booking seldom permits contiguity: a concert in Seattle, then New Orleans, then San Francisco is as likely to follow that sequence as the less taxing itinerary—Seattle, San Francisco, New Orleans. The Trio balk at times and grumble often, but a concert career follows its own sort of logic: you play until they stop inviting you. To a concert manager in New York or Berlin, the strain on the performers is important only by proxy; the booking agent does not need to catch the plane.

The concert season runs, by convention, from mid-September through June. (This has broken down of late, with the proliferation of summer music festivals. Cohen, for instance, spends much of July and August at Marlboro, Vermont.) But if the season be three hundred days, with time for long-distance travel and recording factored in, it's clear that the members of the Beaux Arts Trio spend more than half their professional lives on the road. The creative artist knows no such motion; he does his work at home. And those who perform in a larger ensemble have a more constant base; the opera company or symphony orchestra or ballet troupe has a city affixed to its name. The actor dreams of a long run and some stability in his performing locus; even the popular-music star—with promotional ballyhoo, coast-to-coast junkets, and vast crowds waiting in the stadium—will likely travel less. The soloist or chamber musician, however, makes a living by going on tour, and tours extend in direct proportion to the performer's success.

The paradox of such success is not immediately evident.

Nor are the costs. It is in many ways a hard, repetitive, dull life. Most struggling piano trios would no doubt aspire to the schedule of the Beaux Arts, and gladly trade their ten or fifteen dates for a season ten times that full. In the seven days beginning January 13, 1983, the Trio presented six concerts in France: three in Paris and one each in Besançon, Montbéliard, and Clermont-Ferrand. Besançon and Montbéliard are in the eastern section of France, near the Swiss border; Clermont-Ferrand sits in the Massif Central. The tour was moderately demanding and—in terms of extraordinary incident or circumstance—uneventful. They continued to Switzerland, Germany, England, and Wales, returning to America on February 1. What follows is a day-by-day accounting of one week.

The three Paris concerts take place—on the thirteenth, fourteenth, and nineteenth of January—in the Salle Gaveau. The Salle Gaveau is, by consensus, the queen of the Paris chamber music salons (though some might advance an equivalent claim for the Espace Pierre Cardin or the Théâtre Hotel de Ville). Originally a showplace for pianos produced by the Gaveau Piano Company, the hall is high and sumptuously appointed; its artistic director, Jean-Marie Fournier, has completed extensive renovation. The gilt ceilings have been finished and the loge seats sport new plush. The hall has a display of pianos on the first floor, and office space above; "Le Salon Musical de Paris," as promotional literature describes it, is at 45, Rue La Boétie. The Gaveau Building also houses the Bureau de Concerts Maurice Werner, the Trio's representatives in France. It is a busy season: On the fifteenth, sixteenth, and seventeenth at the hall, Eric Heidsieck, Walter Chodack, and Paul

Badura-Skoda will perform. The Trio's series is devoted to Haydn, Schumann, and Brahms; each of the three concerts includes one piece by each composer.

The men arrive by train from La Chaux-de-Fonds on the evening of the twelfth. For the past several years, they have stayed at the Hôtel l'Aiglon on the Boulevard Raspail. Dominique Werner, heir apparent to his father's concert bureau, collects them at the station. This is more than a mere courtesy, since Parisian taxi drivers balk at the sight of a cello. Werner's black Mercedes can accommodate the musicians, their luggage, tote bags, and instruments; he will play chauffeur throughout the Paris stay. Slender, tall, and affable, with sandy, thinning hair, he practices his English. I compliment his accent and he compliments my French.

My wife and daughters—Greenhouse's daughter and grandchildren—are also briefly in Paris, and we rendezvous for lunch. Since it is raining and chill, we gather in an Italian restaurant near the hotel; the food is third rate. I offer my "musician" joke: Three musicians are traveling through the jungle when their Land-Rover breaks down. A leopard, a lion, and a rhinoceros appear. Because the musicians have read that "music hath charms to soothe the savage beast," they pull out their lute, flute, lyre, sackbut, harmonica, harmonium (I make the appropriate gestures) and commence to play. For its soothing influence, they elect Scarlatti. The lion and rhinoceros sit back on their haunches, entranced, but the leopard appears unimpressed. Midway through the second movement, the animal bounds forward, mauls the musicians, and eats them. This outrages the lion and rhinoceros. They advance on the leopard, tap him on the shoulder, and ask, "Don't you understand anything? Don't you know that music hath charms to soothe

the savage beast?" The leopard turns around slowly, cups paw to ear, and says, "Eh?"

The Trio laugh. Pressler says, "He's deaf!," explaining this to our daughters. Cohen says, "I thought it was supposed to be 'soothe the savage *breast.*'" That's a variant reading, I explain. They are preoccupied with the third Schumann Trio, Op. 110. They have performed it only rarely. The piece is not scheduled until the nineteenth, but they rehearse that afternoon with the emphasis on Schumann, and will do so all week.

The program for the night of the thirteenth consists of Haydn's Trio in A Major (Hoboken XV) No. 18, Schumann's Second Trio in F Major, Op. 80, and Brahms's First (in the revised version) in B Major, Op. 8. On the night of the fourteenth, the Trio present Haydn's G Major Trio (Hoboken XV) No. 25, Schumann's First in D Major, Op. 63, and Brahms's Third in C Minor, Op. 101. On both occasions the audience is large—though less than fully sold out—and vociferously appreciative; afterward the Trio gather in the foyer and sign copies of their records. Backstage, Maurice Werner urges them to hurry: "Every three minutes is fifty records," he says.

Maurice Werner is elegantly tailored and of distinguished mien. He presents his wife. He says he remembers the Trio not from the moment of their first appearance in France—they began under different auspices—but from their first success. The Trio and the Bureau Werner, he says, go back to Divonne-les-Bains. . . . Thursday night he takes the musicians to an after-concert supper where they agree on next year's engagements; they will offer a Beethoven cycle at the Salle Gaveau. He could book them, he confides, far more often than he does; Werner gets only so many days a year, two weeks if he is fortunate, but they have *un succès fou.* There are separate managers for Italy and England and Switzerland and Spain; the European management is based in Germany, and Frau Adler of the Adler Bureau—he says this without bitterness—keeps of course the best dates for herself. There will be a party after the third concert, *chez* Jean-Marie Fournier. "Fournier never does this," says Dominique Werner, but absolutely never; it is a signal honor and I must be certain to come.

After the Friday night concert, my wife and I dine with friends. They have come to Paris in part for the occasion; they live much of the year in the south. I ask my friend—a devoted amateur musician and musicologist—what he thought of the performance. He takes his time responding; he wants to be exact. "Do you remember, he asks, that moment midway through the encore—the Scherzo in Haydn, G Major? That famous instant when the composer pauses, when he opens the door just a little and lets you see the darkness existing, that it *isn't* all sweetness and light? That sudden shift? Well, other groups interpret it either as a mistake, a momentary lapse in Haydn, or they make a focal point, an emphasis, a sudden desperation so that all the laughter dies. But the Beaux Arts"—he pauses—"do just what the composer did; they simply let you see. They present that open door, and then they continue. They acknowledge darkness and then they pass it by." At two o'clock in the morning we are the only customers remaining in the brasserie; we pay and depart.

At nine o'clock I join the Trio for the trip to Besançon; my family returns to the United States. We take the train from the Gare de Lyon, changing at Dijon; it is a three-hour ride. The musicians tell travel stories. They are proud of their endurance, of last-minute arrivals, and of having kept engagements that seemed impossible to keep. Once they had a concert date in Washington, D.C.; they drove to LaGuardia Airport for the flight south. The airport was closed, however, because of heavy fog. They decided to take the train from Trenton and drove there in Greenhouse's car. It was the end of the Thanksgiving holiday. Every seat on Amtrak was taken, and they were not permitted to stand. New Jersey Turnpike travel was bumper to bumper; they crawled south. They arrived in Washington one hour late and played a Mendelssohn trio to an almost empty hall; they repeated the date. Once they missed a concert in Bordeaux because their travel agents had booked them to travel by plane. The airport was closed. When they transferred to a train, there was no way to reach Bordeaux by curtain time; fortunately, the next day was free and they played that day instead. These are the only occasions they have missed. In Europe they try to keep one day free after every five concert dates; in the United States, sometimes they play as many as thirteen days running; it helps to have some margin, Cohen says.

They recollect a flight in New Zealand in a four-seater plane; a bush pilot undertook to get them to an airport where a DC-10 could land. The cello blocked his vision and they had to help him navigate; "Watch the right side," he said. "I hate them wires and trees." Pressler repeats this, delighted: "I hate them wires and trees." Finally they reached the airport; it had only one runway, and the pilot brought their crop duster in, saying, "Not to worry, fellows, good as gold." He taxied to the DC-10, and they transferred planes and flew to Adelaide. Cohen believes it was Melbourne and Pressler believes it was Sydney, but they agree on what the pilot told them: "Good as gold."

Greenhouse remembers in Spain having booked a taxi from a town he cannot remember; they drove all night to Barcelona, three hundred kilometers. On the outskirts of Barcelona, however, the driver panicked; he had never been to the city before and couldn't find the airport; they were due in Majorca that day. He simply stopped and let them out, and they found another taxi and drove on. There are stories of the cello locked in a garage in Dubrovnik, of the cello having been delivered to Berlin instead of Paris as they changed planes in Frankfort; there is the story of the Italian border guard who wanted to stamp the Stradivarius "antique" so it could leave the country with its customs paperwork in order. Cohen tells of a concert in Strasbourg for which they booked a flight from Edinburgh, but Edinburgh was closed. They managed to get to London and get a flight to Basel and rent a car there instead. The only available car was a *deux chevaux*. The car had no heat; it was snowing. Cohen drove. He remembers having missed an exit ramp outside of Strasbourg and ending belly up but off the road in snow. "I can still feel it in my fingers," Cohen says, "the tension of the drive, the freezing chill." Finally they did reach Strasbourg and park across the square and haul their luggage to the concert hall; a large crowd waited in the foyer. No one greeted them or helped them with their bags. They asked for coffee or something hot to drink; there was no coffee available. They asked directions to the greenroom; no one knew. They took a freight elevator finally, and dropped off their suitcases on the wrong floor, and in street clothes, fingers freezing, stumbled out onstage. The concert was a tremendous success, he remembers; they were asked back for next season immediately. He still hates *deux chevaux*.

Cohen spent two months in Besançon after the war. He

studied watchmaking under the GI Bill; he can take a watch apart, he says; it's putting the thing back together that presents a problem. He has friends in the area still; he points out landmarks as we arrive. Two young men meet the Trio at the station, in two cars. One of them hopes to be an anesthetist and one is studying law. It rains. There were floods last week, they say; the river is retreating now but last week was extraordinary. We drive to the Hôtel Frantel. It is nearly two o'clock by the time we register and locate our rooms; the one restaurant available is next to the hotel. Le Casino is empty and ornate; a banquette at the center waits high-heaped with *hors d'oeuvres variés*. We pile our plates deliberately; there are several sorts of herring. Pressler says that Victor Hugo was born in Besançon; there's a statue in the park; Cohen says if the weather improves, he'll walk to the museum on the hill.

The rain is heavy, however. In the lobby of the Frantel, we bet a franc on which of the elevators will arrive first; they arrive at the same time. There are shoeshine machines by the elevator door; the men apply cream to their shoes. They agree to meet at six o'clock; the string players practice, and all of them shower and sleep. I can see the river from my window, the dark high-water mark on the trees; the mist lifts momentarily to show the black stone bulwarks on the hill.

The Saturday program repeats that of Friday in Paris: Haydn's No. 25, Schumann's Op. 63, and Brahms's Op. 101. The Société des Concerts de Besançon presents its two hundred and eightieth concert with an impressively printed program, full of advertisements and photographs; that Pressler's name has been misspelled as "Preisler" seems a minor irritant in the eight-page brochure. The theater manager assures me the hall had been beautiful once; it burned in 1959—the manager conveys suspicion, shrugging his shoulders, lifting his brow—and it has not been sufficiently restored. There are plaster and cinderblock now where there used to be wood, he explains; it was very beautiful once. He is preparing a performance of *The Marriage of Figaro* for the next day; props and backdrops and scenery clutter backstage. The Trio arrive at six o'clock and rehearse the third Schumann for the forthcoming concert in Paris; there are stagehands in quantity, and photographs of the chanteuses and actors and opera stars. Policemen drink coffee and chat. The manager conducts me to the lobby, where I acquire a ticket. My seat has been reserved for the cultural minister; he never comes, the manager explains; his seat is always free.

The cobbles in the courtyard of the theater form a sluiceway; the rain is loud. You should see what happens here in festival time, he says: impossible to find a hotel room in town. The page turner, a girl of nineteen, arrives with her family; they are old friends of Cohen's. The concertgoers are convivial and talkative; an elderly gentleman to my left whistles the theme of the Haydn, regaling his wife with commentary; for the Schumann, however, he sits on his hands. The Brahms is a triumph; people shout and whistle and stamp. Cohen introduces the second and final encore by saying, "*Pour finir . . .*"

Afterward, there is a party at a "*maison typique.*" The doctor who entertains us is, we are assured, of consequence in the Chamber Music Society, a leading citizen of Besançon. His rooms are full of pottery, his floors are oak; the walls have a floral design. My neighbors from the concert are among the guests; they own, it transpires, a castle nearby. The wife approaches the Trio. "I have a bone to pick with you," she says. "You know, it was such an excellent concert, I get fat. My husband gets so excited. When it's a bad concert, we don't eat much afterwards; when it's good we eat a good meal. But if it's a marvelous concert, we simply stuff ourselves with cheese and bread for hours; he gets so excited, he simply refuses to sleep."

The opportunity for such stuffing is available; the host and hostess ply the Trio with Champagne. In a rear room, a table waits with four place settings for "those who have worked"; after a suitable interval, we sit. It appears to be our duty to sample each local meat and pastry and cheese and drink the local cider; I compliment this last. A gentleman in a monogrammed shirt and blue blazer approaches; he gives me his card. He has a daughter in America and a small factory there, as well as one in Besançon and Clermont-Ferrand; he explicates the cider-making process at length. There are issues of fermentation and storage and bottling; the musicians nod, appreciative, and he invites them to his *propriété* to see. They decline. Then the gentleman with the chateau suggests they come to lunch tomorrow; this, too, must be declined. "Perhaps when we return for the festival," says Pressler. "We'll be here several days." A woman who speaks excellent English confesses she failed to hear the concert but teaches English at the *lycée* and would like an opportunity to practice. The page turner inquires if she could be of service for tomorrow's concert at Montbéliard; Pressler accepts. "Sometimes," he says, "you have a physical reaction against a page turner; you know from the moment they introduce themselves that something will go wrong. But this girl is charming, delightful . . ." Montbéliard, an industrial center, is only an hour away. The men had planned to take the train, but the girl offers to drive; she will bring a friend, therefore two cars, and collect us at the hotel. Pressler engages with our hosts to return in the morning to practice; they have a Steinway in the living room, and he assesses it as we say goodnight.

On Sunday the rain slackens, and Cohen and I take a walk. He's gotten used to traveling, he says, and finds a second wind at some point on the tour. But when they start—and particularly after a recording session—he's anxious about the first concerts; the transition is hard. Last night onstage, he still felt as though they should pause and discuss things, as if it were La Chaux-de-Fonds. We stop for coffee in a bar and, twenty minutes later, in a pastry shop; the streets are empty and the storefront shutters drawn. The river is high, and brown; optimistic children dangle droplines from a bridge.

Greenhouse ate too much last night, he says, when we gather once again at Le Casino for lunch. He should have gone straight back from the concert; he did, in fact, return to the Frantel to put his cello in the room and change his clothes. He felt, he says, the strongest desire to stay away from the party, from all that pastry and chitchat and cheese. But the boy was waiting in the hall, and he couldn't disappoint him, and therefore he drank too much cider, and felt sour and sleepless all night. The Montbéliard concert is scheduled for five-thirty; they discuss what to wear. Invariably at evening concerts they wear full-dress suits; they remember making Cohen—when he joined the Trio—buy patent-leather shoes. The Montbéliard concert takes place in late afternoon, however, and they elect dark suits. Twenty years ago, says Greenhouse, they felt they had to dress up to make a good impression; once his wife took the train to Ticonderoga, hours north of New York City, just to bring them pinstripe pants. Those were the years when they drove where they could, driving all night in his ancient Imperial or hundreds of miles every morning to save on ticket costs. He is wistful, weary; he has been on the road since 1955. He travels with one change of clothes and one full-dress complement; he does his laundry nightly in the bathrooms of hotels. A girl at Le Casino, wearing a black off-the-shoulder dress and nothing to hamper her body beneath, tells her companions loudly that she fell asleep at five; this is breakfast, she announces, this Kir and cassoulet.

Véronique, the page turner, appears at the Hôtel Frantel. She introduces her friend, Christophe, a jazz saxophonist, and we pile into the two cars and drive to Montbéliard. Cohen points out the building where he studied watchmaking once, and the bandshell where he had borrowed a violin to play with the park band. The hall in Montbéliard is an eighteenth-century Hôtel de Ville, in an area reserved for pedestrians; we are informed we must park some streets away. The climb is steep; I carry Greenhouse's cello. It rains. Besançon had once been under Spanish rule; Montbéliard belonged to the Duchy of Württemberg, not France, and now is a factory town, dominated by Peugeot. Worried emissaries from the Centre d'Action Culturelle greet us at the door; they had met the appropriate train but found no musicians aboard. Since the Trio had had no name to call, they had not announced their change of travel plans, and those who present the concert are more than a little flustered. We apologize.

Again the Trio rehearse the third Schumann. The program for this afternoon is the Haydn C Major, the Schumann D Minor, and, after intermission, the Schubert B-flat Major, Op. 99. This is the tenth piano trio they will have performed in four days, but the Schubert is a staple of the repertoire and they address it only briefly, warming up. There are many children in the audience, and the concert feels informal. It is a small hall—six hundred seats, without assigned places; children jockey for position while they wait. Someone takes a flashbulb picture at the start of the performance; Greenhouse looks up and scowls. After the Haydn, the *metteur en scène* announces there should be no photographs; the audience applauds. They whistle and stamp for the encores. The Trio offer two: the fifth movement of Dvořák's *Dumky* Trio, and the Scherzo of Beethoven's Op. 1, No. 1.

In Germany, Pressler announces the encores, since his German is native and fluent; in France, it is Cohen who speaks. Once, in Strasbourg, Pressler made the announcement in German, and the audience was shocked. Long ago, Greenhouse remembers, they were in Montreal. In Canada, it is the custom to play "God Save the Queen" and then let the concert commence. Daniel Guilet, however, lost his bearings and began "La Marseillaise." This delighted the French separatists; they had to play both anthems before they could begin.

The reception takes place backstage; there is Champagne once again, and white wine and cheese sticks and nuts. The patrons of the concert society keep the men in conversation until well past eight at night. It is nearly ten by the time we reach Besançon, and the morning train departs at 7:10. Therefore, we forgo a restaurant and agree to meet in the lobby at six; Cohen wins the franc we bet as to which of the two elevator doors will open first. By Pressler's reckoning, the score is six to five.

The morning train from Besançon carries students on their way to school. It is a slow local, with only one first-class carriage; we stuff our suitcases into the overhead racks, obtain a seat for the cello, and settle in; arrival at Clermont-Ferrand is slated for two-fifteen. When the second-class compartments are chock-full, students edge into our carriage; soon they are three deep in the aisle, perched smoking on the armrests, and exchanging extravagant stories about how the weekend went by. The conductor remonstrates with them, not seriously, pointing to the No Smoking sign. We change trains at Lyon, buying sandwich food and a bottle of wine in the station; the second leg of the journey is less crowded and more rapid; Greenhouse sleeps.

Again we are met at the station by two cars; again we arrive at a Hôtel Frantel in the rain. I even the elevator score with Cohen and—counting separate bets as to which side of the train will come into the platform, which door will open—go two ahead. There is a sudden sunburst, and Cohen and I take a walk. We do some desultory shopping—shoes, chocolates, scarves—then enter the cathedral. We admire the stained glass and votive offerings, the statuary, the massive arching buttresses and vault. In the week the Trio spend in France, this will be the single interlude that might be described as sightseeing, the closest any of them comes to a tourist's afternoon.

The program for Clermont-Ferrand consists of Beethoven's *Kakadu* Variations (Piano Trio No. 11 in G Major, Op. 121a), the Charles Ives Trio, and, after intermission, the Brahms C Major, Op. 87. The Ives seems a strange choice. I ask how a "provincial" audience is likely to respond to it and learn that the musical director of Les Amis de la Musique de Clermont-Ferrand requested the piece specifically. "These people," he asserts, "know nothing about modern music. But they have to learn, it is a civic duty. I am myself a classicist, but the twentieth century"—he spreads his hands—"it does after all exist!"

There is much commotion backstage. A guard dog barks; voluble assistants discuss the piano's position, and the angle of the lights, and whether or not they should raise the curtain to reveal the musicians in place. The piano tuner has brought a picnic hamper; after his preperformance "touch-up," he makes a meal in the wings. Doors slam. The impresario introduces me to a series of his students, fondly, calling each "*Ce beau garçon.*" The page turner is a twelve-year-old boy; several members of his family have come with him to watch. The second movement of the Ives has, as musical instruction, "TSIAJ." Ives intended it—as with so much else in his work—to be a kind of compendium of Americana, folk music, anthems, snatches of spirituals, all played at breakneck pace. The initials stand for "This Scherzo Is a Joke"—and the program notes dutifully translate TSIAJ as "*Ce Scherzo est une blague.*" The piece was composed between 1904 and 1911; the Clermont-Ferrand concertgoing public receives it stony-faced. Afterward, however, the musical director is delighted. He cites tunes: "'My Old Kentucky Home,' 'Swanee River,' 'Turkey in the Straw.' Didn't you *hear* them?" he asks.

After the backstage reception, we return to the hotel. We are informed of a restaurant in walking distance that remains open until midnight; it is eleven-thirty. The restaurant has, as motif, a railroad dining car; there are overhead fans and luggage racks, and the cutlery and tables simulate the Orient Express. The meal takes a long time to serve. At the rear of the room there's a bar; the single waiter is also the bartender, and he spends much time chatting, pouring drinks. Someone who appears to be the owner sits across the aisle from us; his own food is served with a flourish. Lanky girls in skintight regalia present themselves as if for inspection, then disappear at the rear. The musicians are restive; it is two by the time we can leave.

The morning train for Paris departs at nine o'clock. The reviews have all been raves. The *Est Republicain*, on January 17, reports on the Besançon concert that took place on the fifteenth. The reviewer begins: "What to think, what to say at the end of a concert of the 'Beaux-Arts Trio' that is not futility?" He then goes on to compare them to the Holy Trinity in their reverend and saintly perfection; he calls them the spiritual proprietors of the music and asserts that "the marvelous perfection of execution surely takes place in the first rank of exquisite things ever heard in Besançon." The review in the same paper, next day, of the concert at Montbéliard—though written by a separate critic—is scarcely less ecstatic. The first paragraph asserts, "One can say without hesitation that the Beaux Arts Trio is the greatest in the world." The reviewer continues: "What life! What enthusiasm! When one hears them play, it is as though they tell us, 'See how simple this is, do as we do.' . . . But it is above all the ensemble of these three musicians that enforces admiration, because they have joy at the same time as nobility, because they tell us, isn't this the human drama?"

The review in *La Montagne,* the paper that serves Clermont-Ferrand, discusses Ives at length. Then the adjectives commence; the soloists are "marvelous," their interpretation was "brilliant and sensitive," they have a "rare homogeneity of ensemble," they "conquered those who listened," they played with and provided "a wild pleasure." Again, the men nap on the train.

Dominique Werner collects us at the platform. Pressler wants to practice at the Salle Gaveau, but there is an interview scheduled with a man from *France Musique.* He is to appear at the hotel at four, and, after a brief lunch, the musicians await his arrival. There has been a misunderstanding, however, and the interview will take place on Thursday—prior to the concert—not this Wednesday afternoon. The men have a free night. Alfred Brendel is playing in Paris, and they attempt to get tickets; Dominique Werner has none. Pressler therefore accepts an invitation to eat in the suburbs with friends, and Greenhouse, Cohen, and I go to a brasserie on the Quai d'Orleans; it rains. The Werner management has inquired if the Trio care to fly to Nice because the night of the eighteenth is open and they could perform in the south. They have refused. Free nights represent expenditures instead of earnings, however, and are rare. The Trio earn, per annum, what a Las Vegas headliner might make in one week's engagement. They are equivalent to corporate executives, not rock stars, and they each remember keenly when the living was eked out. A chamber music group receives, by tradition, less money than a soloist or diva, and their expenses (travel, insurance, managerial commissions, and the like) are high. That Pressler stays parsimonious is impossible to blink; the other two flesh out his tips. He cadges rides and meals. As a guest, he spares no expense. In a small black book he keeps a record of expenditures: who bought the wine at dinner, who hired the taxi or the extra cello seat, who sent the telegram or made the phone call confirming arrival next town down the line. They divide such costs in three.

At the end of one week's touring, I have lost the illusion

of glamour, and say so; Cohen and Greenhouse agree. "But the music," Cohen says, "the chance to play Mozart for a living! The conviction you bring pleasure to an audience . . ." For reading matter they have shared a daily copy of the *International Herald Tribune*. Cohen and Greenhouse take turns with *The Chosen* by Chaim Potok, each losing interest by page 100; Pressler has spent two weeks with a paperback by Robert Ludlum. They have attended no movie, no theater or concerts other than their own; they have gone to no museum or art gallery or park. The mail they have received is manager's communiqués; the exercise they take is sitting down. Their memories are of restaurants and trains. If someone mentions a city, they will say, "Yes, we know it; that's where we had the excellent trout." Or, "Remember, that's where we ate rabbit. Where they drove us to the river, and we were served on a barge." They remind each other, beforehand, of the name of that night's host.

The brasserie we eat in is congenial; Greenhouse says approvingly that the one language he hears here is French. Again it rains. We walk at midnight along the Seine, hunting a taxi; Cohen stops to buy a pack of cigarettes. This is his method of reducing consumption, he says; he never buys a carton but, continually, a pack. Greenhouse relights his cigar. He feels the third Schumann Trio has components of the children's tale, the fairy story, and he wants to stress the playful aspects of the piece. "It's irregular," he says. "But we should give it a try."

They rehearse for three hours next morning. In the afternoon the interview with *France Musique* does take place. The interview is conducted by a young musicologist who hopes to compile a history of chamber music in Europe and America. He brings along an engineer and a female assistant who kisses him at five o'clock and leaves. We sit in an anteroom by the reception desk of the Hôtel l'Aiglon. The questions are provocative; the Trio respond with interest; it is not another piece of preperformance ballyhoo, but an inquiry that deals with their own sense of a tradition. By turns, they speak of their teachers and formative experience: Cohen of Galamian and his work with both the Budapest and Juilliard quartets; Greenhouse of Feuermann, Salmond, Alexanian, and Casals; Pressler of having been principally a soloist until, in 1955, he joined Greenhouse and Daniel Guilet. They speak of the shift to America between the two world wars—how the locus of music making, once firmly established in Vienna and Prague, was driven, with Hitler's help, from the Old World to the New.

"Imagination knows no boundaries," says Pressler. "In principle, you must admit, genius has no borders. Debussy wrote the most Spanish piece in literature, and he never went to Spain. He learned what he knew from a postcard." "And the world has gotten smaller," Greenhouse says. "How far are we from Vienna or Manhattan at this moment?"

Still, there are traditions: Five notes from a trio by Haydn played in Vienna, Cohen says, will not sound similar to the same five notes in a piece by Roger Sessions performed in New York. There is nothing on the printed page, Greenhouse asserts, that will speak to an audience; the music is a contract between composer and auditor, and it demands interpretation—a musician in place who will play. They speak of metronome markings, of the degree of fidelity to a composer's intention it is proper to observe.

They speak of this at length. They have agreed, for instance, to play the opening bars of the Ravel more slowly than as marked. They agree that fashions change. Greenhouse recalls having been moved by a Mischa Elman performance of the Brahms Violin Concerto. He was terribly impressed, he says, by the glissandi, the expressive interludes, the vibrato—but it would sound incompetent today. His present-day students would laugh.

Pressler says, we are not young any longer, we have earned the right to speak with what sounds like pride and conceit. But when we began, a piano trio—as ensemble—was not taken seriously. It was either a poor man's piano concerto or two instrumentalists with an accompanist. But the successful string quartets—he names several: the Budapest, Busch, Amadeus, Juilliard—are not soloists who rehearse for a few hours and give a performance and everyone claps; they have fashioned an ensemble. And now the trio literature is thought of the same way; now it's no longer the poor man's quartet or something to do with one's spare time. . . .

At six o'clock they excuse themselves and dress for the concert that night. The concert begins at eight-thirty and they rehearse for an hour beforehand; the Salle Gaveau is full. The program is the Haydn Trio in C Major (Hoboken XV), No. 27, the Schumann Third Trio in G Minor, Op. 110, and the Brahms Second Trio in C Major, Op. 87. They receive two encores and play the Haydn and *Dumky* they have performed as signatures all week. The *Dumky* is, in essence, a cello aria; if Cohen feels tired, he requests that they play it first. The Brahms brought the house down—or up on its feet, shouting *bis*. The Schumann, however, had been met with respectful bewilderment; it is as difficult to listen to as it is to play. Greenhouse is dissatisfied. "We should program it more often," Cohen says. "We'll try again."

Jean-Marie Fournier lives around the corner from the Salle Gaveau. He and his wife are in the process of renovation at home also—and the gilt work and replastering in their apartment seems almost as extensive as that in the concert hall. The "little dinner" he offers the Trio is a grand affair. We arrive at eleven o'clock, with a half-dozen guests: the Werners, father and son, with their wives; an employee of the Salle Gaveau (a well-dressed, soft-handed, aging gentleman who stopped me when I carried Greenhouse's cello, saying "*Attention*—it's worth a fortune . . ." Later he informs me that his brother-in-law has driven across America, and that once he drove to Vermont; he lives in a residency hotel near the Opéra and detests this weather, he cannot cure the cough); and a German friend of the Trio who happens to be in Paris for the night. Dr. Otto Jung owns a vineyard on the Rhine and regales the Trio there; they have arranged for a seat for him at the concert and an invitation to dinner.

We have drinks in the drawing room. There are amateur oil paintings on the velvet walls—Fournier shrugs: "A relative"—and a Steinway concert grand beside the bar. Dominique Werner's wife speaks English; she and a team of translators—she calls them "*mon équipe*"—are at present engaged on a translation of *The Dream of the Red Chamber*. She cannot speak Chinese, she says, because there is no chance to practice in this town; she wishes next to render Jack Kerouac's *The Dharma Bums* into French. They have two young children and an apartment on top of Montmartre. "It's all right now," she says, "but in the summer, you'll forgive me, there are so many tourists we cannot step out of the house." She comes from a large family and wants at least five sons. Smiling at her tall, thin husband, she asks if I note the resemblance to that other denizen of old Montmartre, Lautrec's Valentin. . . .

The Fourniers are lavish hosts. At midnight we sit to a cold supper catered by Fauchon. There are large porcelain bowls of pheasant pâté at each end of the marble-topped table; the wines have been decanted and the German vintner is invited to approve. He does. We propose toasts. There are fourteen folk at table, and attentive maids. The centerpiece is a cold platter of fowl—pheasant, smoked chicken, and goose—with mandarins and truffles and chestnuts *en gelée*. Fournier—a gregarious, bushy-haired, near-sighted person—keeps saying it is nothing while we praise the food. It affords him great pleasure, he says, to be able to say thank you for the music these three nights. He hopes the Trio will consider, next season, a quick trip to Cannes; they have transformed the casino into an excellent hall. "We fly to Nice," he says. "It takes only an hour. You must be my personal guests." The widow of Robert Casadesus attended the concert, Pressler says; she came backstage and said that the Trio performed like gods. The reason her husband had had no piano trio, she said to Pressler—who repeats this sotto voce to Greenhouse—was that he could find no cellist of such stature. The vegetables are splendidly presented, as are the salads and platters of fruit and ice-cream cakes and biscuits and cheese. Fournier presses cigars on the men, and Armagnac and Calvados and various brandies and marcs. We discuss longevity and the demands such scheduling makes on a performer's physique. Pressler, lighting his Montecristo, asserts that they are fortunate: all other athletes have to retire when young. But a pianist who remains in training can play till he's eighty years old. "Look at Rubinstein," he says, "and Horowitz and Schnabel and Serkin and Arrau." He and Cohen both were born—Cohen one year earlier—on Beethoven's birthday. We drink to Beethoven's birthday, December 16, and theirs. We drink to Greenhouse's birthday, January 1, and turn by turn to everyone assembled at the table with respect to their birthdays and astrological signs.

The Fourniers live on the fifth floor of their apartment building. At two-thirty we leave; Dr. Jung says, since he requires exercise, he will walk down the five flights. The Paris streets are empty, and we make for the Hôtel l'Aiglon at speed. At the Hôtel de Ville, we witness an accident: Two cars bounce off each other. The drivers, unhurt, emerge to argue. "These drivers," Mme. Werner complains. "Even the well-mannered ones are unmannerly behind the wheel. There's no such thing in France as *politesse* with cars." At three o'clock we say goodnight, and Dominique Werner arranges to come back at six. At seven in the morning, the Trio depart for Lausanne. They perform there on Thursday evening, the twentieth of January, and, on the twenty-first, at the Théâtre Musica in La Chaux-de-Fonds. That will mark the halfway point of the year's first tour.

Appendices

APPENDIX A

On September 13, 1983, the Beaux Arts Trio received the Prix d'Honneur du Prix Mondial du Disque de Montreux. This award is given in recognition of career achievement—not, as with the Prix Mondial du Disque, for a single pressing. The presentation ceremonies capped the festival; they took place in the Château de Chillon, on the shores of Lac Leman. The Trio remained—performing twice—in nearby Montreux for three days.

The conductor and author David Blum came to see them at their hotel. He makes his home in Geneva. As a close friend of Greenhouse's and an admirer of the Trio, he responded with kind alacrity to my request for help; he sat the musicians in front of a tape recorder, and asked questions of a more technical nature than those addressed in the preceding individual interviews.

A three-way conversation is as difficult to balance as any other ensemble performance; David Blum, I think, succeeded admirably. I have edited the tapes, since a verbatim rendering would have lacked focus. I have cut redundancies and the infrequent false start. But the conversation here transcribed should be of use to the student of performance technique; it is a welcome addendum. The responses of the

Trio are signaled by their initials, the questions of the interviewer by his own, "D.B."

D.B.: Since the piano is a percussion instrument, many pianists have difficulty simulating a *legato*; on the other hand, string players often lack clarity of articulation. What means do you use to reconcile these intrinsic instrumental differences?

M.P.: There are ways in which a pianist can create at least the simulation of *legato*. One has to want, to imagine it; one must sometimes rephrase a passage. I try not to attack the keys suddenly, but to have the wrist come down into the instrument; the hammer itself then comes down at a controlled speed, slower than usual, and that eliminates the percussive quality. Of course, the pedal too can help. I would use the kind of pedal that is closer to Debussy—a precise degree of release that is not quite complete, that breathes with the musical line without breaking it.

D.B.: Is it not true, also, that in order to simulate a *legato*, the note following a long note must be a little softer than the beginning of the long note?

M.P.: Yes. One must adapt to the natural diminution of sound. The art is to make use of this diminuendo and, by means of a subtle crescendo, take the moving line and build it back again little by little until the full sonority is restored.

D.B.: From the string players' point of view—you who can very easily make a long singing line—how would you help your articulation when you need enhanced clarity?

B.G.: To a great extent it's a question of bowing, of having a vital bow-to-string contact, of using the most appropriate bow stroke: a *spiccato*, a *martelé*. . . . We also use the left hand as an enunciating factor, which means a little bit of percussion simulating the piano percussion. We must take care to emulate the clarity of the piano sound—for instance, in rapid passages.

I.C.: Very often, for example, *staccato* dots over a series of notes will sound rather shorter on the piano; then it behooves us to change the kind of bow stroke we use. We have to try to match each other. But it's a two-way process; often we will find that the dot's too short, or we come to another conclusion, that the dot's too long. And sometimes even in a *legato* passage we may alter a bowing, depart from the written indication, because of the diction, the clarity that may be required.

M.P.: It's important to emphasize the point Izzy just made. Whether the piano rearranges something to suit the strings, or vice versa, it's a function of matching; it has to be worked out so that the instrumental textures blend as closely as possible.

D.B.: To what extent does articulation on the cello differ from that of the violin?

B.G.: The main difference would be that it takes a little bit longer for the lower strings to respond to the bow. I always have to be careful not to lag behind the violin sound, which is much more direct. And so I very often will create an attack just a split second before the violin, so that the sound will seem to come from the instruments at the same instant. The thickness of the string itself means that the sound is going to be a little bit postponed, especially on the lower strings of the instrument; there's less difficulty with the top string, the A. Left-hand percussion helps to create an immediate response on the C or G string.

D.B.: What of intonation; how much can the violin and the cello use "expressive intonation"?

B.G.: It's perfectly possible to play with expressive intonation as long as you're not doubling a part with the piano. The moment there's a doubling one has to conform to the piano; otherwise one sounds out of tune.

I.C.: The burden is on the string player because we can adjust. Even if the piano hasn't had a first-rate tuning, we have to adjust to it when we perform. There's also the question of balance, and this is often related to the register in which we're playing. I find the lower the range, the greater lack of clarity; the high notes come through, but the low ones need particular attention.

D.B.: What must the pianist particularly look out for in creating a balance with the violin or the cello?

M.P.: That differs from composer to composer. For instance, if we play a Haydn trio, I'd play the bass notes lightly, knowing that they're doubled by the cello. This would be true for Mozart also; I'd use as little pedal as possible, with the intention that the predominant timbre would be that of the cello. The piano should merge into the cello sound instead of the cello merging into the piano sound—as is sometimes the case, for instance, in a "romantic" work. There should be no fat on the side of the sonority.

D.B.: Which composers write with a rather thick texture?

M.P.: This already starts with Beethoven. He was of course

writing from a pianist's point of view—so he might indicate a *fortissimo* for all the instruments, even though the string players have the leading voice. So you must adjust for that. Right in the beginning of the *Geister* Trio, for instance, the piano must give the effect of a *fortissimo* but not actually play it. There must be no sacrifice of the sense of power, but it must arrive through the meaning of the phrase. With Schubert the orchestration is already better; he is easier to balance. And so is Mendelssohn. Schumann is the most difficult of them all.

D.B.: Which composers best understood the piano-trio medium?

I.C.: That's a difficult question because there are works which present tremendous problems in texture and balance, but which are nevertheless among the greatest. In Opus 70, Number 2, for example, Beethoven pitches the strings in a fairly low register, which presents problems (except for the occasional flourish in the violin, or a cadenza-like section for the cello). It tends to sound rather muddy and cloudy. There's a great difficulty in achieving clarity and balance, but as a piece of music it is absolutely marvelous. The third Schumann Trio, the one in G minor, is another example. As a piece for performance, it presents great difficulty and doesn't seem to go over well. But as music we feel—certainly in the slow movement—that it's sublime.

M.P.: A piece of perfect writing for the trio medium is the first movement of the Ravel. It's utter perfection; he uses the three instruments as one unit; they complement each other.

B.G.: I think Brahms—more than any other composer—understood the form of trio writing. He understood it even better than Schubert—who gives, comparatively, a lesser part to the piano.

D.B.: What would you say are the most demanding works in the repertoire—from the spiritual or the technical standpoint?

B.G.: I would mention the opening of the Shostakovich Trio, with its harmonics, as being one of the most nerve-wracking experiences in the repertoire.

M.P.: To me, the most difficult are the Beethoven Trios—not from the technical point of view, though the *Archduke* is a major operation for the piano. But Beethoven combines technical difficulty with such an enormous emotional demand. . . .

I.C.: For me, the Ravel is very difficult: the second movement with its alternation of notes played with bow strokes and left-hand *pizzicati*, its extensive use of harmonics, and the third movement, where he demands unity of color by playing on one string. . . . And I think we agree that all three of the Schumann Trios are very demanding, the last two in particular.

D.B.: Would you comment on the relationship between the printed score and the living performance? What aspects of a score are by their very nature ambiguous?

I.C.: I think of the mark *dolce*; it can mean many things. First of all, one must consider the dynamic context in which it appears. Then, is it sweet saccharine, is it sweet reflective, is it sweet as in the morning sunshine? These are all very personal meanings which are expressed by the interpreter; the same *dolce* can never have exactly the same meaning for two people, and I think this applies to many written indications.

B.G.: It's also true for tempo markings. Furthermore, certain rhythmic groups have a particular character which can't be notated. One has to understand above all that it's a matter of re-creation; it's up to the conscience of the performer to come as close as possible to the composer's intention. A printed score—unless it's brought to life by a musician who can interpret it—conveys no more than a pale image of a work.

M.P.: To me, the score is just like a map, the map of Switzerland, for example. When I arrive in the country, I get the map and it's then that I begin to travel. I take a musical score, reflect on it, and discover where I find myself happiest, where I can express myself strongly. The work must be done within that personal context; satisfaction comes through a personal relationship to the score. One can to a certain extent make it in one's own image, too. Even though this sounds sacrilegious, one is not only responsible to the composer; one is responsible also to one's *love* for the composer. After many years you come to the point where the work becomes personal, and you feel a certain something that may not agree with accepted opinion or the way the score is marked. We may even sometimes change a tempo from that which the composer had indicated. Naturally we almost always do exactly what's marked—but I'm thinking of an exceptional case—the first movement of the Ravel. Despite the *modéré* tempo marking, he adds a metronome indication—the eighth note at 132—that conveys the impression of a dance which goes rather quickly. Yet for us, the movement has an unhurried, nostalgic, a bittersweet feeling. The tempo changes with the character—but I don't feel we misrepresent the composer.

I.C.: Just to continue that for one moment, I find that even in music in the twelve-tone school—where you sometimes find five or six indications as to how one single note should be played—you will start perhaps with a *forte*, a *piano*, there will be a crescendo, then a diminuendo, and in between it will say *molto vibrato*, and then a further dynamic at the end—even then, where you have so many written indications, there is still the element of what it means to you, and you must still interpret all these marks. It's only a blueprint, and we digest it, and by the time of performance it should have attained a new meaning.

M.P.: In chamber music the line is always drawn between your ability to be free and your necessity to be bound. Because you can only lead to the extent to which you will be followed, and you can only follow to that extent to which you accept the other's leadership. So there is a fine line that cannot be transgressed in a good ensemble; otherwise you'll end up with a war and not collaboration.

D.B.: Could we turn our attention for a moment to the question of vibrato?

B.G.: Where we have to be really careful is in finding the same quality and character of violin and cello vibrato where we play together or repeat similar phrases. My feeling, however, is that for many string players today, the vibrato has become almost an automatic hand reaction—motorized. There tends to be not enough variety in the way it's produced. Vibrato should help with the emotional content of what one would like to project. I think that an enormous variety in vibrato is possible—and it has to be thought of in conjunction with dynamics. A vibrato can help with the phrasing; it can do as much as a crescendo to increase intensity.

I.C.: And we have to have some similarity in the concept of the basic sonority of the piece we're playing. The spirit has to be stylistically adjusted; the vibrato for Haydn can't be the vibrato for Schumann. The exploration of the kind of vibrato that is to be used, for example, in a French piece as opposed to a German romantic piece, as opposed to a piece of Bach—these are things which I find, on the part of young people, to be a little bit slighted. That's a very important part of interpretation; one could give a marvelous performance of a Bach sonata, but if one uses what I would consider a romantic or a Russian vibrato, then it may be ruined.

B.G.: One has to be careful with this non-vibrato, however, because when you stop the hand completely from any movement, you have no life to the sound. And that becomes a bit boring; you're just playing notes without any expressiveness. Sound has to be alive whether you're projecting a serious phrase or one in a happier mood.

I.C.: I don't disagree. But at the beginning of the slow movement of the *Geister* Trio, for instance, we use a barely perceptible vibrato—and that, too, expresses something.

M.P.: And don't fool yourself; the piano can vibrate. There

is a vibrato; I hear it. Perhaps it's a sympathetic reverberation to the string vibrato, perhaps it's a spiritual entity—but I do hear it.

D.B.: How does the interpretative element form and develop within the Trio?

M.P.: We try. Everybody has ideas, and very often the ideas are the same, or perhaps only two of us will have the same idea; then we adjust, we talk, we argue, we try. And it may come down to the point that we can't agree; then we decide it should be performed one way or the other.

I.C.: For example, there are fourteen bars of *sforzandi* in the first movement of the *Archduke*—and there's a question: Do these *sforzandi* imply an increase in dynamics as they go along, or should they really come down in a diminuendo—in order to emphasize the *fortissimo* at the end? I remember when I first joined the Trio, I thought the former, and the others thought perhaps the other way—so we decided that for two performances we'd do it one way, but on the third we would try the other. I find that to come to the first rehearsals and to be rigidly fixed about what the work means is a mistake—because it really involves an interpretation which has to be evolved collectively. It's a mistake to come to those early sessions thinking you've solved the problem; this is how it is and ought to be. The other way is time-consuming, but eventually you have something which is perhaps greater than what you could manage for yourself.

B.G.: Over a period of time we can be amazed by our own early recordings, to the point where we don't even recognize a performance as one of ours. That has happened in the past. We've listened on the radio to one of our early recordings, and our ideas have changed so substantially that we haven't even recognized it.

D.B.: Could you mention areas where you feel there are significant gaps in the Trio repertoire?

B.G.: The first thing I can think of is that we have a very limited amount of repertoire with orchestra. I'd certainly like to see more contemporary works for the Trio—particularly with orchestra.

I.C.: One area that's sadly neglected is the beginning of the twelve-tone school—Schoenberg and Webern, Berg. Bartók and Stravinsky also produced no piano trios, and that's a shame. It's also unfortunate that the music written today is so difficult for amateurs—because it requires extensive study before you can put together your own part, let alone that of a group. You can't just sit down and play music that's being written today. The advent of the phonograph record, of course, has decreased the demand for house music. If Beethoven wrote a symphony, and it was a success, then the publisher immediately put out a transcription for four hands, for quartet, quintet. . . .

D.B.: What points of advice do you most frequently find yourselves offering young chamber musicians?

B.G.: Stay together. I'm not referring to playing in tempo, but to the commitment to remain in an ensemble together over a long period of time. Even when a chamber music group is formed in a university atmosphere, the first thing that may happen is a clash of personalities, and the desire to insist on one's own ideas—so that groups sometimes fail to last longer than a semester. You should pick people who will stay together, not just for an evening or series of evenings.

I.C.: From a technical point of view, the young groups I listen to are usually very fine. But from the point of view of projecting the music and conveying to the listener an emotional experience—from that point of view, often something's lacking. They themselves need to make sure they understand the emotions involved in the music; perhaps they are afraid to express themselves; perhaps they're not quite sure what the composer meant to express. There's a historical background to the music. There are stylistic facets that must be explored. The young person today can go to many teachers; he can go to concerts, he can listen to recordings, both historical and contemporary, and this is a great source for obtaining knowledge of both repertoire and interpretation. But it's then up to the student himself. No single teacher provides all the answers. He must search for the relevant material; he must acquire the feeling of having been an intimate of the composer, so that when he does interpret the composer he says, ah, I know what he was up to here; this, I believe, is what he wanted to express.

M.P.: I always try, when I coach a young performer or group, to tell them where I find the great moment in the piece, to share my secret with them. It *is* a secret, after all, a different point of reference from those who came before me, and it may very well be different from those who come after me. I share that and try to show them that point, to express what I feel when I play it—it may be no more than five bars. And then I say, now, you select your own five bars . . . .

B.G.: Each of us in his day has had an idol. And I think that it's also important for the young musician to pick someone who is a very fine artist in the field and to copy the things which he finds to be very beautiful, because there is a continuance in this life of ours from one generation to the next. And the things that one artist from an elder generation has experienced should not be lost to the younger. As time goes on, there are changes in the way in which we perform—but great artistry should not be lost. It should be assimilated.

APPENDIX B

As indicated in the chapter on recording, the members of the Trio rarely are explicit in discussions of technique. As Bruno Giuranna put it, "When musicians must discuss the piece, it's a very bad sign. You should have it in your head, of course, have considered it all in your head—but you must play with your heart." Nonetheless I urged the Trio to "consider it all" explicitly, and to offer close analysis of an agreed-on text. After some time we settled on the first movement of Beethoven's Op. 70, No. 1, the *Geister* (Ghost) Trio. What follows are transcriptions of three tapes.

The musicians did not confer. Cohen and Pressler call it a "bar," Greenhouse a "measure"; Cohen likes the Henle edition more than do the others. I have let these little dissonances stand. So, too, with the larger, since they seem to me to represent the variety of strategies deployed by the three men. Cohen was the happiest with this form of scholarship. Greenhouse viewed it as, principally, a physical exercise—where Beethoven demands energy of the performer, where restraint. Pressler undertook it as a kind of coaching session, instructing an imagined pianist in the problems posed. These pages are studied most profitably in conjunction with the score.

Isidore Cohen: The First Movement of the *Geister*

We're discussing Opus 70, Number 1, by Beethoven, the first movement, which is marked *allegro vivace e con brio.* I would use an edition which would be as accurate with what Beethoven wrote as is possible to find—at the moment that for me is the Henle edition. The opening tempo, I would say, would be about sixty to sixty-three to the dotted half note or to the bar. The opening five bars should be stormy, tempestuous, as forceful as possible. In the first bar, in the second beat, where we have an A and a G, I would not honor the slur which Beethoven wrote there, but for reasons of clarity and strength, I would separate the A from the preceding notes in the slur so that the beginning of the bar would be down-bow, the A would be up-bow so as to match, to honor Beethoven's dot and to make sure that that A in the first bar is heard clearly. In the following two bars I would accent a little bit the notes which give the intervals of the sixth and the seventh; in other words, in the second bar I would have an accent on the B and on the D, and also on the G in the third bar. After the first four notes, going back to the beginning of the piece, I would make a crescendo which goes from the first bar and continues through until the fifth bar—a feeling of crescendo, that the line is rising in intensity. In the seventh bar, the *dolce*, the second part of the first theme which is started on the F sharp in the cello, there is no indication there of a dynamic change in either the cello part or two bars later in the violin part. However, that *dolce* connotes for me a dynamic level which is either *piano* or *mezzo piano*, in contrast to the violence of the opening *fortissimo* of the piece.

In bar 18, I would make absolutely sure that one does not make a diminuendo before the *subito piano*. I would save enough bow so that I can continue the crescendo to the very last minute and make sure that vibrato is there, so that the piano in the nineteenth bar comes as a *subito piano* exactly as Beethoven wanted it. In the nineteenth and twentieth bars, those eighth notes in the strings should be short. There are no dots on those notes, but I would play them as if there are dots. In bar 26, the last two eighth notes in the violin part, E and D, I would consider perhaps changing bow and breaking the slur, which is in Beethoven's original marking, for reasons of leading into the *fortissimo*; I feel that the phrase leads into that *fortissimo*, and that possibly the slur would make those two notes weak. It can be done as written, but I would also try to change bow on those two notes in the twenty-sixth bar. In bar 27, there's a danger for the piano chords in the right hand of overbalancing the cello part in bars 27, 28, and 29, and then the following bars where the violin starts to play and both cello and violin continue; those piano chords in the right hand from bar 27 on must give the impression of great strength, but the pianist must make sure that he does not overbalance the strings there. In bar 29 going into bar 30, I would give the impression of a crescendo-diminuendo in the groups of six notes which occur in each of the voices, in the violin parts and in the cello parts; that is, a crescendo going to the bar line of bar 30, then a feeling of a tiny bit of relaxation, so that each of those groups goes to the fourth note of the group. In bar 33, in the violin part as well as in the cello part, Beethoven has six notes slurred there; that is, the last three notes of 33 are slurred into the first three of bar 34. Because of the strength required in the *fortissimo*, I would play those as three notes to a bow, and then three notes to a bow, and then ending in bar 34 again, as written with three notes to the bow. I think that the bowing indications do not permit sufficient strength as written. In bar 37, the third beat, and in bar 38, the third beat—where the violin has chords with the piano—there again is a problem of balance. If played too heavily, they will not permit the cello part—which I feel should be heard and is at a slight disadvantage because of its range—those chords in both the violin as well as in the piano have to be treated lightly. Again, the problem is to give the impression of strength and energy but not to overbalance the cello.

For the second subject, which begins in bar 43, I think the strings must give the impression of a very very light scale line, and what we do is we play *flautando*—it mustn't be exaggerated, but the effect should be one of complete transparency. It should not be the usual sound produced in *piano*, but should be a more delicate, a more transparent sound to be achieved by moving the bow a little faster than normally and a little lighter than one normally would. In bars 49 and 50, at the end of the line of the cello and violin, I would give a hint of a little bit of a swell and then diminuendo there—we're reaching the end of a phrase, the phrase has arched up a bit, and I think it should have a feeling of coming up and then relaxing to the cadence in bar 51. Now the second subject in the violin and cello in bar 52 is marked *piano*, and we have just come from a *piano*, but this *piano* which is in bar 52 is no longer the same kind of *piano* which we had starting in bar 43. The *flautando* now is discarded—we have a firmer *piano*, a *piano* which has more body in its sound. And in bar 52 I think that one must make absolutely sure that the sixteenth note at the end of the bar in both the cello and violin is distinct—it must be heard. There is a danger of it passing by inaudibly, and it must be clearly enunciated. That, of course, applies wherever this second subject is presented in this same form—that would be in bar 52, in bar 54, and then all the following sixteenth notes must be treated with the same care so that they will be heard. In bars 56 and 57, the second quarter note in each of those bars played by the strings, I would make more than normal effort to continue the crescendo through those notes. In other words, the tendency to drop the second note of a slur must be fought against so that, for example in the violin part, the D in bar 56 must certainly be stronger than the E—the second beat must be stronger than the first, and in the following bar, again the C sharp must be stronger than the D—to be done by a combination of bow, pressure, and vibrato. In bar 60, we have a one-bar crescendo, and in bar 61, we reach a *forte*. Now that's a tremendous dynamic change, and special effort must be made that the crescendo come up immediately, so that by 61 we have reached a *forte*. It's a swooping, a very fast increase in intensity of sound. In bar 62, there's a delicate ensemble problem. The last sixteenth note in that bar played by both the cello and violin can present a little bit of a problem. The cellist and the violinist must be in good eye contact and make sure that that sixteenth note is together. The same applies, of course, in bar 65—the last sixteenth in that bar, too, requires special care so that the ensemble is absolutely together.

Now starting bar 70, we have a rather unusual mark—

it's three *pianos* for the dynamic range in all the instruments. Despite that I would still, in bars 72 and 73, the last two bars of the first section, I would try to carry out the feeling of a diminuendo even from that triple *piano* so that one has the feeling of music which is receding and receding and finally is practically gone—barely audible. And then, of course, the repeat must be made.

We start now the development section, bar 74. We have the idea of the first subject being used here, only now it's in *pianissimo*. It should be played simply, lightly, and perhaps it has an element of playfulness in it now. It used to be something which was terribly tempestuous; now its character has changed completely. To that end, in bar 77 in the violin part, I would bow it starting up bow on the two sixteenth notes, and then including the D which is in the second half of the second beat in the same bow, so as to try to contribute to this feeling of lightness and perhaps playfulness. I would use the same bowing pattern in bar 81 in the violin part. In bar 82, that *subito fortissimo* should come as a shock, as an outburst; there must be absolutely no hint of it in bar 81. In bar 88, we have *piano* in all three parts; that is, the dynamic *piano*. I would not play so soft there, the reason being that four bars later, in bar 92, we have a *pianissimo*, and I think that in order to make sure that we can distinguish between the *piano* of 88 and the *pianissimo* coming up later, I would change the *piano* in 88 to that of *mezzo piano* to give me enough sound so that I can drop in bar 92 to a softer dynamic: the *pianissimo* that Beethoven demands. Now the phrase beginning in 92 is a very difficult one to manage in the violin part. It involves some awkward intervals, but yet it should be accomplished without any hints of slides between notes. The sound for the four bars starting 92 and going to bar 95 should be as even as possible—you must avoid any hint of a crescendo or diminuendo in that line. Here I have a feeling we need an absolutely straight, flat line. Now these phrases which begin at 92 and then continue until bar 108 are difficult to manage in the bowing as suggested by Beethoven, which is four bars slurred. Still, whenever it is at all possible, I would attempt to do the four bars in one bow as Beethoven asked. If in the course of a performance I find that I am running out of bow and it's absolutely essential, then I will change the bow. But I will do my damnedest to try to get all four bars in in one bow, as Beethoven prescribed. Bar 107, the last quarter in the violin part, presents a small problem. We mustn't give away the *forte* of bar 108. The tendency is to make a crescendo on that note and lead into the *forte* of 108. So what I would do is limit the bow—I would start it as an up-bow, very close to the frog, and use very little bow on it so that I can come crashing down on the *forte* in 108. Now, in 108 there is a quarter-note motif followed in 109 by a triplet motif. Now the triplet motif tends to come out sounding much stronger, having three times as many notes as the quarter-note idea, so I would equalize the ideas by playing a rather strong *forte* in 108, and then I would play something between a *mezzo forte* and *forte* in 109. I would also lighten those triplets in 109 by playing them slightly off the string. This idea I would carry on for ten bars or so following in which this idea keeps recurring. The lightening of the triplet, I think, will also work to my advantage when we arrive at bar 120 where suddenly we are demanded—Beethoven asks of us—to play *fortissimo*, and this idea should be heroic, broad, as fat a sound as possible. I think the easing up on the triplets in the preceding section will make it easier to achieve that in bar 120.

Bar 128 starts a tricky area for ensemble again. The right

hand of the piano and the violin play the same rhythmic figure and are playing in harmony, while the cello, starting two bars later, has the same motif with the piano but this time with a *piano* left hand. Now the ensemble there must be very carefully watched so that the notes are absolutely together between, on the one hand, the violin and piano and then left hand, piano and the cello. I would also do as I did at the very beginning of the piece—use this motif beginning in bar 128 in a crescendo; that is, I would play the first beat and the following eighth in *fortissimo*—but then I would start a crescendo, which would take me through to the end of the motif, that would be starting bar 128 and, in the middle of that bar, dropping a bit and then making a crescendo to bar 130. And I would follow the same pattern again in bar 132, going with a crescendo until bar 134. In bar 140, again we have this same motif which is being used and developed here, but here I feel that absolute steadiness of rhythm must be maintained, because the figure is going around and around in all three voices and sometimes in two voices, and it must be maintained at an absolutely steady tempo so that there is no feeling of freedom here; almost metronomic is what we need. Starting bar 145, there is a difficult section between piano right hand and the violin. There is a diminuendo of a fast little figure that requires special care so that the two parts are together. What I do in a case like that, of course, is play practically by memory and watch the pianist's hands so I can be as much together with him as is humanly possible. In the *pianissimo* starting bar 149, each player must be particularly careful that the motif of eighth note and two sixteenths is heard in its *pianissimo* dynamic, but right after that the notes are softer, whether it be in the cello, in the violin, or in the piano, so that that motif can be forever present and not interfered with by any of the other notes.

Right before the recapitulation, which is bar 157, I would say it would be possible to take a little sniff of time on the last one or two eighths before 157 as if one is taking a gasp of air before plunging into cold water. It perhaps can be done without taking time, but we prefer to take just a little bit of time, and as soon as we start bar 157 right on the downbeat, we go back immediately into *tempo primo*. Of course, all those ideas which we presented at the beginning of the movement concerning first subject, second subject, etc., apply here in the recapitulation because so much of the material is the same. However, when we come to bar 173, which is dealing with the second part of the first subject—the quiet part, the *dolce* part—suddenly we find ourselves in the key of B flat, and that section beginning 173, it seems to me, is tenderer, is more loving, is calmer than that subject was ever presented before; and so I would reflect that in the way I play those bars. In bar 183, we are still dealing with the same second part of the first subject, but we have now an *obbligato* that runs in the right hand of the piano part; and the way we in the Beaux Arts Trio present this section is that I don't play *pianissimo* as written in bar 183, but I play two bars in the dynamic of *piano* and then drop in bar 185 to *pianissimo*. The effect is one of two bars, let's say, dominated slightly by the violin and then the *obbligato* in the piano in bars 185 and 186 emerges. Then this pattern is repeated in the next two bars where the violin again will come up and then again recede to let the piano part come through, and once again the idea is treated in that way, except that in bar 194 we make a definite diminuendo—the reason for that being that the sequence of the *obbligato* and the theme the violin is playing, starting in bar 183, seems to build up in tension; it rises first, starting on D in the violin, and then in bar 187 starting on E flat, and then rising again in bar 191, starting on F. There is a natural feeling of growth, of crescendo, and we must somehow come out of that crescendo in bar 194—therefore, we make a diminuendo in that bar—so that 195, where Beethoven says crescendo, starts at the quietest possible *pianissimo* level.

In bar 216, we are again in the second subject. Here, part of it is presented by the cello and violin as it was at the beginning of the piece. But then in bar 224, the idea is given to violin and piano. Now I will match my sound to that of the cello in bar 216, and then when I play the same material—though different notes, of course—in bar 224 with the piano I must change my color, my texture. Of course, in bar 224 we are in a crescendo, so that already makes for new demands on the instrument, but the colors that I must use with the cello are different from those which I use when I play with the piano. Bar 245, the end of the bar especially, presents a problem in catching the piano at the end of its three-bar run of sixteenth notes, which is descending and is sometimes not very very clear, so that the arrival on bar 246 at the triple *piano* is very difficult; and I think the string players must be particularly careful to watch and to listen to the pianist so that they can arrive at 246 together.

Our coda begins at 250, and there we take a slightly more relaxed tempo; the music demands it. In bar 253, I use a slightly fancy fingering—that A in bar 253, I use a harmonic on the A string—the reason is I want to get as light, as transparent a sound as possible. Also in bar 253, I will slightly hold back the tempo even though we have started already a slightly more relaxed tempo; there I feel the need of even more relaxation. And then in the section which begins in 254, we will gradually come back to tempo; imperceptibly at first, but by the time we reach the crescendo in bars 262 and 263 and 264, there we will really start to accelerate, so that by the time we reach the final statement in bar 268—the final statement of that first opening motif—we are back to *tempo primo*, and the last two chords must be played with the greatest energy and the greatest strength to end this rather tempestuous and monumental movement.

Bernard Greenhouse

The edition with which we must confront Beethoven is the Henle edition. I find, however, that in publishing an edition of this kind, the editors have gone back to a source which in many respects carries through errors that might have been corrected via later scholarship. We had become accustomed to hearing editions such as those provided by C. F. Peters—and the very few notes changed still come as a shock to my ears. Nonetheless we use the Henle *faute de mieux*—and, in terms of the *Geister* Trio (Op. 70, No. 1), it does seem adequate.

The first piece which I ever performed with a chamber music group was, in fact, the *Geister*; I was fourteen years old at the time. The performance was attended by John Erskine the writer and then president of the Juilliard School of Music. In conversation with Erskine after the performance, I came to the decision to continue with chamber music and also to attend Juilliard. And each time I perform the piece today, I remember the excitement and thrill of playing this work when young; it still feels like a debut.

To begin with the problems of the first attack: each violinist has his own means of indicating to the cellist when the attack begins. There are violinists who nod their heads, and then a split second later have the bow on the string. One must become accustomed to the habits of his colleagues—the string colleague in particular. To be able to catch that first D in the first measure sometimes is a problem. Occasionally the piano will cover up a multitude of sins, but if one has played for a while with the violinist, one knows that the nod of the head doesn't necessarily mean the beginning of the first note—the first D. The next problem would be one of being able to raise enough sound in the *fortissimo* to match the great sound coming out of the piano and the higher register of the violin. Therefore, it takes much effort on the opening to contribute the *vivace* and *con brio* and still be heard as a cellist. The second very difficult moment in the opening of the *Geister* Trio is the change in emotional content which is necessary when one reaches the F in measure number 5—the change is completely up to the cellist; he must create a change from the *vivace e con brio* to one of *dolce* in measure 7. The sustained sound on the first measure—measure 6—and the diminuendo and change of emotion on the second measure—measure 6 of the F—forces one to sustain the bow in measure 5, and then suddenly to drop sound and change the vibrato as well, in order to indicate the change from *con brio* to *dolce* in measure 7. In measure 8, there is a choice of either staying on the A string from the A to the C sharp or crossing the string to the D, playing a harmonic D and then going back to the E on the A string in measure 9. I have always chosen a fast movement of the hand from the A to the C sharp rather than crossing strings, which creates a change of sound color that I'm not particularly happy with. But the slide must be avoided; it's possible to do a fast shift.

The next problem would be in measure 20—to coordinate with the violin on the two eighth notes in *piano* and then the *subito forte* in measure 21. We go on to the *fortissimo* in measure 27, where the cello has a major voice in *fortissimo* and must actually battle with the sound of the piano at that point in order to achieve the leading voice on the eighth notes. From measure 35 on, of course, the cello has the leading voice, in a register which is quite difficult; it takes great energy to bring out the line—35, 36, 37, 38, 39, 40, and so on—all of that passage until 51 takes an enormous amount of strength of sound and the maximum that the cello can produce. Then we have in 52 the *subito piano*. I like to play the sixteenth note a little bit longer in 52—also in 54—and the crescendo must build until the *forte* in 59 with a little bit of a lean on measure 60 on the A. A slightly slower feeling in the upbeat to measure 65, and then once again the tempo in measure 66. The problem in the *pianissimo* in measures 70, 71, 72, and 73 is, again, to obtain an ensemble with the violinist, simply because the bow doesn't always attack the string exactly when one wants, and one must be extremely careful to match the quality of sound on the As, which we have in unison with the violin. Visual contact at this point is essential.

The problem of starting in measure 74 is considerable. I have come to use the open A string for the beginning of the second half of the movement. It's extremely difficult to catch the tempo, and I feel that the open A is a clearer announcement of the passage than playing on the D string with a fourth finger—from the A to the G sharp, for example. Using the open A string, I find that I can play in the exact tempo that has preceded this measure. Going on, I try to get, in measures 76 and 77, as *legato* a feeling as possible, a feeling of lightness and airiness in the *sempre pianissimo* in 78 and 79. The *subito fortissimo* in 82 must be enormously powerful again, in order to contrast with the *sempre pianissimo* which has preceded this. We want a fine *legato* in the *pianissimo* in 92, and that should be done with great care and together with the violin—so as to continue this wonderful feeling of *legato* and *misterioso*, through, actually, measure 108. At this point, we have the first indication of a change in dynamic level; we have a *forte*—all this preceding period has been *pianissimo* and as *legato* as possible. Then we have the *fortissimo* in 109, which continues with a roughness of attack, the *sforzando* in 113, and again the *sforzando* in 115—all this with great vigor and energy—and 119, again, the *sforzando*, with a final fling with the bow in measure 120. The cellist then has a chance to rest for a few measures until again he's called on to produce the maximum that the cello can give in measure 125. Here there is a wildness in Beethoven's writing; I don't believe, in 128, that there should be a separate change of bow after the sixteenth notes to the eighth, so I tie the A, B flat, and C together, the same in measure 129—I tie the two sixteenths with the eighth. All this is enormously energetic with a feeling of great anger and vitality throughout the section—134, 136, 137.

The change comes in measure 147 where the diminuendo starts. From a *fortissimo* in the preceding section—the maximum sound—suddenly we must make a diminuendo which lasts only for two bars and brings us to a *pianissimo*;

and the difficulty is to make clear the eighth and sixteenth notes in measure 149. What I do is actually separate the A from the two sixteenths, the C sharp, and the B. The *legato* is marked in that measure, but I make the separation there, and also in 151 in order to clear the sound of the instrument.

In 153, we have the *subito fortissimo*, again with renewed energy. We must be careful in 155 to match the tempo of the violinist in this passage. I think the problem rests more with the violin and the piano than with the violin and the cello because the cellist is able to watch the violinist's bow and then coordinate, while the violin is concerned with keeping the ensemble with the piano at this point. In measure 156, the last eighth note is sustained a little bit longer. There is a break before we start in 157, and this presents a problem of timing; the length of the break, of course, becomes important. We return to the theme in 157, and this is essential to rehearse because of the difficulty of ensemble. In 161 and 162, we have the same problem as with the very opening theme; there is a change of character from enormous anger to *dolce* in two bars.

The last time we have that *dolce* in 173, I sustain bars 171 and 172, providing a slight hesitation before going into 173; this expresses a change in the thematic material. Beethoven has written the *dolce* for the last time, and I think that at this point, it's most important to show in some way this last change, and to do this I sustain a little bit more in 171 and 172 before continuing on with the *dolce* in 173. It's the slightest bit of hesitation, and I think it brings out this last change.

We go on: we have a period of *pianissimo* in 183, which continues until we again find the crescendo in 185 to 199—the same energetic *forte* through this entire section until we have the *sforzando* in 207. We have had most of this section in the opening of the piece. Now we come to the very end—the coda. We must be very careful as far as ensemble in 246, 247, 248, and 249—these measures are very, very difficult to get together with the violin, and one must be completely aware of the bow of the violinist rather than the nodding of his head in order to be exactly with him, since there is a unison which is extremely important for ensemble. The coda, the second ending, must have a calm that reflects the *dolce* section. There must be an attempt at minimal sound at the point where it's marked, in 254, *sempre pianissimo*, a continuation of the sound—no inflections, no rising of the dynamic level—so that the crescendo which comes at the very end, the gradual crescendo leading from 262, to the *fortissimo* in 268 with the *forte* in 266, 267, is enormously exciting; what we do in the Beaux Arts is actually to begin a forward motion in 262 in order to help the feeling of crescendo, so that by the time we have reached the finish, the last three bars—268, 269, and 270—it's almost an impetuous feeling at the very end—the *fortissimo* is again of maximum strength.

To review the difficulties of the first movement of the *Geister*, I would say that the energy and sound required to make the cello part an important part of trio writing is substantial. I would say the changes of emotion within a short time span, energy for the opening, take a building up and a burst of energy; the *dolce*, too, in measure 8—the ability to get from the A to the C sharp without an ugly slide, to present that *dolce* in a manner that is not supersweet but carries out an idea of Beethoven, which is not one of real *dolce*, possibly, but one of sadness. And then we have, in 35, the necessity for articulation in that entire passage; I use the left hand to the greatest possible advantage in bringing out the clarity of that passage, which goes on until 51—I think that is extremely difficult. Another major difficulty is the start at 74 in the *pianissimo* where the cello is alone with the piano. These are a few of the places I think about before we start to play the work; I have in mind the preparation necessary to bring them out. The ensemble difficulties are in the back of my mind, so that I'm prepared for them before they occur. Technically, I would say that the first movement of the *Geister* is not as difficult in many respects as the second movement, where control of the bow is so essential. Ensemble, the feeling of keeping a tempo, becomes really a challenge to the chamber music performer. The first movement is one of pent-up energy for the cellist—not terribly difficult as far as the actual production of cello technique.

Menahem Pressler

Each time when I look at the beginning of Opus 70, Number 1, the first five bars seem to be like an uncoiling of a spring; I personally, physically, take a deep breath before starting to play those bars—conscious of those inner accents like downbeat, the G in the second bar, the B, the D, the E, the F. It should be played in one breath. Then, with the B flat in the sixth bar, in the bass—that transitional bar which Beethoven is so fabulous at—in one bar, the whole outlook seems to change. And here I find that although it says *piano* in the piano part, I do play it with a lean on the B flat, so as to find a release when the A comes in the seventh bar.

In the thirteenth bar, I am very careful as to balance. I take over from the strings the melodic line and yet continue with the crescendo, which in itself is a kind of intensity; there seems to be no end. I do feel that the last triplet in bar 18 has to be played *forte* so that the contrast in the nineteenth bar, the release, is felt. Also, in the twentieth bar, those two octave As in the left hand, the second one should be very light, so that a feeling of diminuendo exists. In bar 23, I do try to break my chord in conjunction with the violin chord so that we both come together. In bar 27, those chords that are in *fortissimo*, I play them *fortissimo*, and at the same time use very little pedal in order to make the cello solo cut through; yet one must keep the strength and character that those chords imply. They're always offbeat, and therefore they enhance the urgency of this phrase. I advise great care in bar 35 at those *fortissimo* places because the cello lies in a poor register. We must not cover it but at the same time give it the impetus it demands; so I play it strong, yet with an ear at all times to be able to hear the solo voice.

Observe with care the left hand in bars 61, 62, 63, and place the sixty-fourth bar so that it resolves. I'm very conscious at bar 67 of keeping both hands clearly together; although it starts already with *pianissimo*, one should aim for a continuous fall in dynamics—that means one should have a feeling for a diminuendo, which goes all the way through to the very end of the exposition—the last A octave. Bars 74, 75—very careful with the *legato* in the left hand, which is an absolute contrast to the motif of the beginning that the cello starts, and which the piano continues and the violin finishes. And each time that occurs—

in bar 78 again—I'm very careful to keep it as much *legato* as possible, then not to make a crescendo in order to have as much contrast for the *fortissimo* in bar 82 to come in. Also, I'm very careful at bar 88 that the *piano* is a singing piano, careful to sustain that melodic line all the way until a *subito pianissimo*. There I try to be as close to the keys as possible, an even tremolo in the right hand and the left hand going with the outline of the leading line, which is the violin part. Also, when it continues, I practice very carefully those tremolos in the left hand of the piano that can become cumbersome, can become fat or thick. One has to be absolutely in good practice and the weights in the hand have to be divided so evenly as to make those tremolos what they have to be—transparent, a kind of shimmer. Be careful in bar 108 not to smudge the last two sixteenths of the bar, in order to get ready for the response in 109 where one responds to the strings' attack. Careful that the attack is not too loud, because, after all the piano can overbalance at this point when it plays with maximum strength. Always in the bars that have those sixteenths, listen very carefully to those last two sixteenths (of bars 108, 110, 112, etc.). Careful when entering bar 121 that the strong *fortissimo* leads into the second bar, into 122, but not with an accent, just with a rich sonority that is complementary to the string sonority. The same should be true in bar 124, when the left hand of the piano takes over the line.

In bars 128 to 138, the rising line is to be played in crescendo and the falling line in diminuendo. But since the crescendo is in the right hand and then is given to the left hand while the right hand goes down, each pianist will have to practice carefully in order to be capable of going first with the violin line up and then with the cello line up and with the violin coming down. It's quite difficult and takes practice because during this furious tempo and intensity of playing, one has to have prepared in such a way that one is capable during that time still to observe those difficulties it presents to each hand alone. One ought to pay attention to the *sforzando* in 141 and not do it in 143, although the same phrase continues. In bar 149, lean a little bit into the D sharp in the left hand; have the sense of intensification, somewhat of a crescendo, so that in bar 150 it can again run out or run down. The same in bar 151—that D sharp—a slight lean. And again in bar 152, run out so that the *subito fortissimo* which starts it is played with great vigor and strength.

I would advise that in bar 155 one begin with the sense of starting anew and leading up in strength to 157—so the cadence that goes into the theme is like a climax. And then again, of course, bar 157 must be played in one breath up to the high F. Place the B flat again clearly so that again it will prepare in as short a time as Beethoven has given here for the entrance of the *dolce* theme in the cello. And be very careful that two bars later, the piano has the sense of continuity with the cello part; the weight of the arm should be freely hanging into the key, so that one achieves sonority without punching down the keys. I try to give the F and the Bs in bar 172 a special lean, meaning that one is capable of achieving a color change for 173 when the cello takes over and the violin continues. Then at 176, 177—the upbeat to 177—the piano takes over that line on the same level and intensifies it more and more and more until the diminuendo; all this should be as melodic as possible. And here from bar 183, one should play each of those sequences with a different color. I try to bring each one down so that when one gets to the crescendo—bar 195—that is truly the low point; be very careful with articulating the left hand so that there is, after all, the freedom of the right, which has triplets, and then four triplets, and then six triplets and five. This is a very fluid, beautiful passage or scale line, and the freedom implied even rhythmically has the fundamental support of the left hand. In bar 199, again be very careful, as in the exposition: look loud but don't play too loud. In bar 207, take over with the right hand the line that the strings have given you, and continue to bring it down into piano. Think of it in terms of melody, so that when the sixteenths come, as in bar 211, they are not thrown away but clearly enunciated. Careful with the crescendo starting at 224—careful so that it has enough strength and intensifies up to bar 235 and reaches a climax there. Then, again, as in the exposition, place the left hand from 237, 238, 239 into 240, which should be placed to achieve a sense of reaching the tonality of G, although it's only in preparation for the last arpeggios. And, again, those arpeggios down, from bar 243, should be very carefully felt as if they create a diminuendo. Then when it comes to the second ending in bar 250, I always try for a kind of sonority that has a peaceful illumination. Now how does one achieve that? One has to conquer all weight in such a manner that you enter the keys with only the natural weight of the hand—no pressure, but just having the arm, the hand, go into the keys, and that in *pianissimo*. Bar 254, we carefully take over the line from the violin, and find the E minor in bar 258 as a low point, like the second before the outbreak of the storm; for me, this is something very special and something I practice for, or look at and listen to, in order to achieve that certain kind of relaxed and clear sound which, again, is a matter of arm weight distributed just right. Bars 266 and 267: be careful, just one *forte*. And bar 267, that violent *fortissimo*: be careful that the two sixteenths in that bar are clearly enunciated and played, and drive those to the very end in *fortissimo*. Yet at no time bang or hit the piano, because the *fortissimo*, too, has to go only as loud as the two strings can go.

It is difficult to do Beethoven's extreme full justice, especially in a chamber music setting. Yet, on the other hand, it is also that challenge which enables one to do it well. One should take a chord and play it repeatedly in *pianissimo* up to its maximum *fortissimo*—and yet make sure that at no time is it just a barely hit chord. How can one judge the right tempo, the *allegro vivace e con brio*, for this movement? I guess it is how clearly one can in speed enunciate, how clear the passage work can be, and how transparent it can still be. I do believe that *allegro vivace con brio* does demand real speed. It's not a *presto*, yes, that's all right, it still has to keep being an *allegro*, but within the meaning, in the frame that he gives us in this movement, the tempo in itself is a vital factor in being able to give back the meaning of this movement and express its impetuosity.

APPENDIX C

The Beaux Arts' itinerary for 1983–84 is representative. It includes five tours in North America, four in Europe, and a brief visit to the Far East; they perform 127 concerts. I do not include time budgeted for rehearsal—generally, the days prior to appearance with an orchestra for, say, the Beethoven Triple Concerto. Nor do I include sheer travel time, such as the flight from Amsterdam to Hong Kong; the dates listed here are only those on which the Trio perform. They each maintain teaching schedules, in addition, and give guest performances elsewhere.

For the sake of brevity, I do not name the concert halls or programs—nor which of these performances is a "Festival." "New York" could therefore mean either the Metropolitan Museum Concert Hall Series, the Brooklyn Academy of Music, or the Mostly Mozart Festival. The frequency of concert dates in Washington, D.C., reflects the fact that the Trio are, this year, "in residence" at the Library of Congress. On the October tour, in the two-week period from October 10 to 24, the Beaux Arts will play twenty different trios; that, too, is representative. The following is the text of a Telex sent by Hattie Clark to the Trio in Switzerland on September 14, 1983. It gives some notion of the range of the almost daily decisions as to scheduling:

WOULD YOU CONSIDER DOING COMPLETE BEETHOVEN TRIOS SAN FRANCISCO ANY TIME BETWEEN MID-JUNE AND END JULY 1985 AS PART BEETHOVEN FESTIVAL AND IF SO NUMBER OF CONCERTS IT WOULD TAKE. AT PRESENT THIS AN INQUIRY BUT IF AGREEABLE WILL PURSUE. ALSO CASALS FESTIVAL PUERTO RICO ASKING ABOUT CONCERT VERY EARLY JUNE 1985. ALSO GRAPPA WANTS TWO WEEKS 84–85 BUT SEEMS IMPOSSIBLE TO PROJECT UNLESS TRIO THINKS OTHERWISE. ALSO FLORIDA MUSIC TEACHERS ASSN MEETING JACKSONVILLE WILL TAKE NOV. 3, 1984 PLUS SEPARATE MASTER CLASSES FROM EACH NOVEMBER 4 WHICH DEAN OWEN SAID HE DISCUSSED WITH MENAHEM. . . . FLORIDA GAINESVILLE INTERESTED HAVE YOU DIRECTLY AFTERWARD, SHOULD WE ENCOURAGE? AS YOU KNOW THIS PERIOD OUT OF REGULAR TOUR TIME AND YOUR EUROPEAN TOUR COMMENCES NOVEMBER 12. REMINDERS: FOR RAVINIA HOLDING JULY 23 THROUGH 29, 1984, NEED ANSWER FOR CARAMOOR. ALSO IN VIEW HOLLE TELEX OF LAST WEEK AM I RIGHT IT SEEMS SAFE TO HOLD AUGUST 25, 1984 FOR SOUTH MOUNTAIN? REGARDS, HATTIE.

September	7:	Köln
	9:	Edinburgh
	10:	Biarritz
	12:	Martigny

	14:	Montreux
	15:	Besançon
	16:	Pontarlier
	17:	Dôle
	18:	Aldeburgh
	19:	Aldeburgh
	20:	Aldeburgh
October	10:	Cambridge
	11:	Providence
	13:	New York
	14:	New York
	15:	Purchase
	16:	Ottawa
	17:	Toronto
	18:	Toronto
	19:	Toronto
	20:	Sewanee
	21:	Columbia, Mo.
	23:	Ann Arbor
	24:	Chicago
November	12:	Haarlem
	13:	Utrecht
	15:	Lübeck
	16:	Köln
	17:	Leverkusen
	18:	Frankfort
	19:	Fulda
	20:	Bonn
	22:	Southampton
	23:	Abbotsholm
	24:	Belfast
	26:	Belfast
	28:	Yverdon
	29:	Zurich
	30:	Biel
December	4:	Montreal
	8:	New York

9: New York
10: Cambridge
11: Randolph, Va.
12: Pittsburgh
13: Johnston
14: Daytona Beach
15: Miami
16: Fort Lauderdale
17: Purchase, N.Y.

January 9: Valencia
10: Alicante
11: Santander
12: Paris
13: Paris
14: Paris
16: Avignon
17: Avignon
18: Brussels
19: Antwerp
20: Wiesbaden
21: Eindhoven
22: Amsterdam
24: Rotterdam
25: Niemagen
26: The Hague
27: Amsterdam
29: Hong Kong
30: Hong Kong
31: Hong Kong

February 9: Washington, D.C.
10: Washington, D.C.
11: Rockville
12: Rockville
13: Cambridge
14: Charlottesville
16: Washington, D.C.

	17:	Washington, D.C.
	18:	Columbus
	19:	Baltimore
	20:	Montreal
	22:	New York
	23:	Washington, D.C.
	24:	Washington, D.C.
March	1:	Washington, D.C.
	2:	Washington, D.C.
	3:	Lincoln, Neb.
	4:	Omaha
	5:	Kansas City
	8:	New York
	9:	New York
	10:	New York
	11:	Quebec
	12:	Hamilton
	16:	Poughkeepsie
	17:	New York
	18:	New York
April	1:	Ventura
	2:	Tempi
	3:	Palm Springs
	4:	San Diego
	5:	Pasadena
	6:	Santa Barbara
	7:	Berkeley
	8:	Portland
	9:	Seattle
	10:	Vancouver
	11:	Denver
	12:	Boulder
	13:	Salt Lake City
	15:	Northampton
	16:	Cambridge

May 28—June 7: Recording,
La Chaux-de-Fonds

June	10:	Darmstadt
	11:	Darmstadt
	13:	London
	14:	Redding
	15:	Nohan
	16:	Divonne-les-Bains
	17:	Divonne-les-Bains
	18:	Divonne-les-Bains
	20:	Strasbourg
July	22:	Bloomington
	23:	Ravinia, Ill
	24:	Ravinia, Ill
August	25:	South Mountain
	26:	Caramoor
	27:	New York

As of August 28, the Trio are in Salzburg and commence 1984–85.

APPENDIX D—DISCOGRAPHY

The majority of the Beaux Arts Trio recordings have been made for Philips Records. A division of Polygram—other divisions include Deutsche Grammophon and London Records—the Philips label contains all but three of the earliest disks in the Trio's repertoire. Those three are as follows:

Composer & Selection		
HAYDN:	Trio No. 1 in G Major	MGM Records, E-3420
MENDELSSOHN:	Trio No. 1 in D Minor, Op. 49	
FAURÉ:	Trio in D Minor, Op. 120	MGM Records, E-3455
RAVEL:	Trio in A Minor	
DVOŘÁK:	Trio in E Minor, Op. 90 (*Dumky*)	Concert Hall, M-2323
MENDELSSOHN:	Trio No. 1 in D Minor, Op. 49	

The Beaux Arts now record exclusively for Philips, and, as Chapter V suggests, continue to expand their listings. I am indebted to Peter Clancy of Philips for the Discography here provided. The designation "MC" signifies "musicassette"—a term evolved to prevent confusion in shipping and manufacturing between "Kassette" (German for "box") and "cassette" tape.

Composer & Selection		LP	MC
BEETHOVEN:	Piano Trio in E flat (after the Septet, Op. 20), Op. 38	6514.315	7337.131
BEETHOVEN:	Piano Trio in D (after Symphony No. 2) Trio Movement in E flat	410.3761	410.3764
BEETHOVEN:	Complete Piano Trios	6725.035	7655.035
BEETHOVEN:	Piano Trios, Op. 1, No. 3 & Op. 70, No. 2	6514.131	7337.131
BEETHOVEN:	Piano Trios, Op. 1, Nos. 1 & 2	9500.988	7300.988
BEETHOVEN:	Piano Trios in B Flat, Op. 11, *Gassenhauer* & in D, Op. 70, No. 1 *Ghost* (Digital)	6514.184	7337.184
BEETHOVEN:	Works for Piano Trio; Op. 44, Op. 121a, *Kakadu,* WoO 38, WoO 39	6514.279	7337.279
BEETHOVEN:	Complete Piano Trios	6747.142	
BEETHOVEN:	Concerto in C for Violin, Cello & Piano, Op. 56, London Philharmonic Orchestra/Haitink	9500.382	7300.604
BEETHOVEN:	Piano Trio No. 6, *Archduke*	9500.895	7300.895
BRAHMS:	Piano Quartets (Complete) Walter Trampler, viola	6747.068	
BRAHMS:	Piano Trios	6770.007	7650.007
BRAHMS: BEETHOVEN:	Trio in A Minor, Op. 114 Trio in B Flat, Op. 11 George Pieterson, clarinet	9500.670	7300.826
DVOŘÁK:	Piano Trios, Op. 21, 26, 65, 90, *Dumky*	6703.015	
DVOŘÁK:	*Piano Quartets,* Op. 87 & 23 Walter Trampler, viola	6500.452	